Climbing Out:
Grand Canyon Hikes 1997-2006

by

Robert C.A. Goff

Dreamsplice
Christiansburg, Virginia

Climbing Out: Grand Canyon Hikes 1997 -2006

Copyright © 2019, 2023 by Dreamsplice

All rights reserved, including the right to reproduce this book, or portions thereof, in any form.

Image credits:
Richard M. Goff   *[RMG]*
Robert C.A. Goff   *[RCAG]*
Paulette Hardin   *[Xena]*
Andrew Morikawa   *[AM]*
Adam Tawney   *[AT]*

Map credit:
The snippets of topographical maps marked to show the course of each trek are from the Trails Illustrated (National Geographic) map for trails of the Grand Canyon (1994 revision), derived from the USGS maps of the area. [For planning of hikes, a current version of the Trails Illustrated map is recommended.]

Dreamsplice
3462 Dairy Road
Christiansburg, VA 24073

www.dreamsplice.com/books

Cover design by Robert C.A. Goff, Copyright © 2019 by Dreamsplice
Front cover photo by Ralph Jones (GCNP)
Back cover photo by Adam Tawney

ISBN: 979-8-9867728-3-7
Library of Congress Control Number:2019911360

First Edition: September 2019
Revision 2: November 2023

Contents

South Bass-Hermit Loop   4
   November 1997
   Bob and Micah (8 days)

"BB9" Tanner-Indian Garden Loop   29
   December 1998
   Bob, Micah, Richard, Andy, Paulette (10 days)

South Kaibab to Clear Creek   69
   January 2001
   Bob solo (5 days)

South Kaibab to Phantom Ranch   91
   December 2006
   Bob, Richard, Andy, Paulette, Mike, Adam
   (4 day "codger hike")

South Bass-Hermit Loop, November 1997
Bob and Micah (8 days)

About the Hike

The Bass-Hermit loop involves vehicle travel to a remote trailhead, followed by hiking in a remote portion of the Grand Canyon. The road is impassable following rain or snow. The Tonto Trail between Bass and Hermit is like a toaster oven during the summer. The seasonal water at Serpentine and Ruby is unreliable. Even perennial water has been difficult to obtain at Turquoise on some occasions. If you get into trouble in this stretch, help is a long way off. But it is the very remoteness of the trek that I found so alluring.

[2019 NOTE: In this day of cell phones, I have no idea if there are any cell towers accessible along this remote portion of the Tonto Trail.]

Our timing was fortuitous. Heavy rains and floods three weeks prior to our trip primed the aquifers, allowing nearly every side canyon to greet us with flowing water. The interval between the rains and our trip permitted the quagmire of the roads to Pasture Wash Ranger Station to solidify and dry.

Climbing Out: Grand Canyon Hikes 1997-2006

Itinerary

Date	Course	Distance	Water
11/3/97	Ride to S. Bass trailhead with off-duty Ranger S. Bass trail to river	7 miles	bedrock tanks, river
11/4/97	Bass Rapids to Serpentine Creek	4 miles	seasonal *tinajas* (route to river)
11/5/97	Serpentine Creek to Ruby Creek	5 miles	seasonal *tinajas* (route to river)
11/6/97	Ruby Creek to Turquoise Creek	6 miles	perennial (route to river)
11/7/97	Turquoise Creek to Slate Creek Side trip down Slate to Crystal Rapids	12 miles 2 miles	perennial (route to river)
11/8/97	Slate Creek to Boucher Rapids	7 miles	perennial (route to river)
11/9/97	Boucher Rapids to Hermit Creek	7 miles	perennial (route to river)
11/10/97	Hermit Creek climbout to Hermits Rest	7 miles	Santa Maria Spring
7 nights **8 days**		**53-57 miles**	

Micah and Bob at the trailhead [Ralph Jones]

In the Supai.

Day 1: Monday 11/3/97

Cloudless sky and a crisp, autumn wind greeted us, as we unloaded our gear at the Hermit Trail parking area shortly after 7 a.m. We had awakened at 5:45 to get packed and drive out the West Rim. With eight days of food and water, my external frame Kelty pack weighed in at 60 pounds. We would leave our car here, to reclaim at the end of the hike. As previously arranged, my son, Micah, and I were met shortly by Ralph Jones, who was to drive us to the South Bass Trail head. Jones had told me the day before that the road to Pasture Wash was in "perfect" condition. I had been aggressively conditioning for this trek since the previous January. Micah, at age 19, had seen no need for such preliminaries. Since my age was nearly fifty, I decided that I would need all seven days of hiking prior to climbout to comfortably ascend Hermit Trail.

The roads leading to Pasture Wash ranger station seem to exist in two states of navigability: horrid and impassable. After a rain or snow, according to Jones, a car simply sinks into the mire, never to be seen again. Even though I frequently drove my 1984 Bronco II over jeep trails and abandoned roads in the Appalachians, I was impressed by the drive to Pasture Wash. Potholes excelled in both depth and raggedness. Only Jones' skilled driving avoided frequently bottoming out on the rocks and ridges in mid-road. Some seldom mentioned features of this drive are the lack of water sources along the way, and the fact that, even by straight-line, skilled compass navigation, it's a twenty mile hike back to GC Village, if your car has a serious problem. When the road is wet or snowy, a traveler in distress can pretty well count on encountering no fellow humans along the way. The road being "perfect" today, we jostled our way to the South Bass trailhead in about an hour and a half. We pulled in beside a van already at the trailhead. Apparently our immediate predecessors were still in the Canyon.

Ralph Jones snapped photos of me and Micah at the trailhead sign and also with Mt. Huethawali in the background. Once we had said our good-byes, we were committed to walking back to our car, left at Hermits Rest. We began, bolstered against the chill wind by fleece hats, jackets and Thermax longjohns.

Micah in the Hermit Shale.

The descent to the esplanade was fairly straightforward, first entering the head of Garnet Canyon and crossing over the saddle between it and the head of Bass. Views up river are spectacular here. We acquainted ourselves with the Coconino-tipped, Holy Grail Temple, which would stand above our hike for the next several days. Along this stretch, we met Chris Everett (owner of the van), a professor of photography at Northern Arizona University, with a companion (? wife). It seems that professor Everett is on a sabbatical to take pictures of the Grand Canyon. (It's a dirty job, but somebody's....) Then we lost the trail alongside Mt. Huethawali. We had stayed too close to the rim of the esplanade, instead of veering closer to Mt. Huethawali. In this portion of the trail, it is necessary to stay on trail in order to locate the notch leading down to the Supai. Five minutes of wandering located the trail again. After descending the esplanade, the trail turns sharply southward and continues to the head of the Redwall in Bass Canyon. It was

Wheeler Fold in the Bass Formation.

atop the Redwall here, that we encountered two river rafters, one carrying a small day pack, the other hiking in Tevas. They were planning to reach the esplanade via a climbers shortcut, which simply zooms up the head of the canyon, then return to their camp below Bass Rapids by following the trail down which we had just hiked. We wished them a good hike, not realizing that they would be the last people with whom we would speak for the next five days.

The descent of Bass is steep and brushy, but the easiest Redwall descent I have done. Below the Redwall, we stayed high on the East, most of the way, despite the temptations of numerous alternate routes cairned within the creekbed. The creekbed routes tended to be strenuous boulder hops, rather than the tedious, brushy contouring of the trail higher on the slope. Any of the routes will get you down the Canyon, the differences being the effort required and the number of thorn scratches sustained. Lower Bass seemed to go on forever, with its spooky, dark red and black walls, and its relentlessly clawing brush. Tonto West and, further down, Tonto East were clearly marked by larger-than-average cairns above the Tapeats. We never did see the lower, shortcut to Tonto West. Temperatures hovered in the seventies on the Tonto. Stagnant water was present in the bedrock tanks.

Cactus garden along the Wheeler Fold.

At the bottom of Bass Canyon, the falls bypass is clearly cairned. Clarity of route is not the problem. It is the descent from this bypass trail to the beach below Bass Creek that is hard to accept. After climbing down from the rim, this final, short, fifty-yard stretch of "trail" is, in fact, an easy climber's route to the beach. Descending it with a sixty-pound backpack on wobbly, Jello-thighed legs is a sensation only to be experienced, not to be described. Just before reaching the sandy beach, we passed the abandoned Ross-Wheeler, towed up onto the rocks by William Wallace Bass himself.

Both of us were thoroughly beat up by the time we reached the sandy beach. Micah took the first piece of level sand. I walked on down to below the falls, hoping a house-sized boulder didn't shoot over the edge if it rained during the night. It had been cloudy earlier, but by the time we reached the river, is was only a little hazy as the sun set and the stars began to appear. I prepared buttered noodles (forgot to add the oil) with fragments of dried beef. Banana cream pudding for dessert. Both of us sat by the MSR Whisperlite stove in a stupor of fatigue. I succeeded in not thinking about the climb up from the beach tomorrow. Filling our 4 and 6 liter MSR Dromedary bags in the river was something of a nuisance in the dark. We treated the water that night, and for the remainder of the hike, with Polar Pure iodine. We learned over the course of the hike that the Dromedary bags are most easily filled using a dip cup, rather than trying to immerse the bag in the water source. The appropriate iodine solution for each bag was put into my drinking cup, then added all at once to the bag. Dishes were washed with plain water and scoured with fingers only. Each of us carried a Lexan spoon, a plastic bowl and a plastic, 1-cup drinking cup (Micah's having calibrations marked on the side).

Inner gorge and Colorado River at Bass Rapids.

In addition to our Dromedary bags, each of us carried a 1 liter Platypus with a drinking tube attached to the pack shoulder harness. These worked out very well in encouraging frequent drinking. Mine tended to leak at the bite valve if I left the hose filled with water. So after drinking, I would blow the water in the hose back into the collapsible bottle. By the end of the hike, both of us agreed that the Platypus was a good idea, but the volume of one liter is a little small, requiring a pack-off break to refill the Platypus. I think that some way to attach the drinking hose to my six liter Dromedary would be great.

This was the first of many evenings on which I leveraged my solid walnut, hand-carved, Marsh-Wheeling Deluxe Stogie walking stick over a boulder and suspended my food bag from its wrist loop. In low use areas, which includes most areas west of Boucher, only a pocket mouse will succeed in climbing out the walking stick and down to the bag of food. (In the heavy use areas closer to GC Village, mice, packrats, squirrels and ringtails maintain their own Special-Ops teams to overcome all but the most impenetrable barriers to reaching your food.) Micah, too lazy to rig a pole from which to hang his food bag, adopted the frowned-upon practice of keeping his food inside his pack, and his pack inside his tent at night. From Bass through Boucher, he encountered no problem with critters trying to reach his food. (At Hermit Creek, he saw the wisdom of being more cautious.) With my food out of my pack, I simply unzipped all its compartments and pockets, covered the entire pack loosely with a pack rain cover, and left it standing against a rock overnight. Although I found an occasional mouse dropping inside my pack the following morning, I had no problems with damage to the pack or any of its contents—with the exception of the Ziploc in which I stored my entire roll of toilet paper. For some reason, mice nibbled on that Ziploc, though not the paper within, on several occasions.

Micah applies moleskin at Bass beach.

On the subject of toilet paper, NPS regulations require that you pack out your used toilet paper when hiking in wild areas. We solved this interesting challenge by each carrying a wide-mouth PET plastic peanut butter jar in which to carry the used toilet paper. Before beginning the hike, I crushed a toilet tank chlorination tablet within a Ziploc bag, then placed half of it into each jar. Throughout the hike, the jar emitted only the odor of a swimming pool when opened. The jars were neatly tossed into a dumpster at the hike's end.

Micah's tent on the beach of Bass Rapids.

Day 2: Tuesday 11/4/97

During the beautiful, balmy night, the Colorado rose about one and a half feet, and became a bit muddier. In retrospect, we camped a little close to the river's edge. Next time we camped on a beach, we moved a little farther from the river. The climb up the bypass was painful and exhausting. By the time we reached the Tonto East junction, both of us could hardly walk. Up was alright. Down was excruciating. Once again, I failed to see the junction for the shortcut to Tonto West, despite looking intently for it.

There was something strangely uplifting about leaving the dark walls of Bass Canyon behind us. The Tonto Trail to Serpentine was easy enough to follow. Serpentine Canyon, verdant and bright, radiated a friendly, almost welcoming aura. The Tonto on the western side of the drainage seems to boulder hop through about a dozen strenuous side drainages. Serpentine is a long canyon. I worried all day about whether water would be near the Tonto Trail. The canyon bottom appears to be a long excursion of sand and boulder nests all the way to the river. Several sources state that it is possible to reach the river down Serpentine, but neither of us had the energy or enthusiasm to add a four mile round trip to the river at the end of the day's hike. I was overjoyed to see water gently flowing in Serpentine, just where the Tonto trail crosses.

Micah enters Serpentine on the Tonto.

Micah with a fossil rock in Serpentine.

After setting up my Eureka Timberlite tent, and Micah his Eureka Timberline, both on a rock ledge above the creekbed, we explored up canyon. We found incredible fossils: large slabs of crinoids and stems;

Flowing water at the Serpentine trail crossing.

one two inch ellipsoid object, almost like a rose bud. (Aside from the caloric expenditure of hiking out with such fossils, it violates NPS regulations to remove them.) Micah prepared an excellent dinner of Creamy Garlic Shells (with dried beef) and vanilla pudding.

Herringbone clouds cleared the rim just at dusk. I wondered if it might snow tomorrow.

Micah prepares dinner in Serpentine.

Day 3: Wednesday 11/5/97

I awoke at first light. Although the air temperature was in the upper 30s, the rock slab upon which we slept radiated heat like an electric blanket beneath the sleeping bags. The day was cloudless and blue. The day's hike would carry us from Serpentine, past Emerald, Quartz, and end at Ruby, the last of the "seasonal" water sources we had to contend with.

Micah and man-eating limestone.

Emerald Canyon is not hiker friendly. Many side drainages, with boulder hops and ups and downs sap your strength. There is a giant chockstone at the head of Emerald, where the trail crosses the main drainage.

Bob on the Tonto.

The climb out of the drainage is difficult. The creek was dry.

Quartz is much kinder. There are gobs of fossils all along the canyon. At our lunch break, Micah created a collection of about three dozen curved, finger shaped fossils. I called it the Ten Minute Fossil Collection. All were collected within an area of about 200 square feet. Micah left them arranged beside a shady overhang. Like Emerald, Quartz was dry as a bone.

Bob's golden agave headdress.

Micah's 10 minute fossil collection.

Ruby is a spectacular canyon! It is the longest canyon I'd seen, with receding, misty promontories stretching several miles back, with the south rim showing through a notch at the head. It suggests a fantasy land of mysterious wonders, each side drainage more

Micah on a boulder at Ruby.

secret than the last. Again, as in Serpentine, water flowed just above the Tonto Trail crossing. We considered hiking to the river, but wandered up canyon instead, enjoying the shade of cottonwoods and tall shrubs. The canyon is so richly blessed with riparian flora and signs of fauna, it is hard to believe that its water ever dries up completely. I searched diligently for maidenhair fern, to confirm my suspicion that its water is perennial, but found none. That doesn't prove that Ruby is not perennial, but it certainly leaves the question open. Regardless, several sources confirm a path to the river in Ruby, with a cairned bypass of the fall to the East. While I searched for maidenhair, Micah scoured the bouldered creekbed for rattlesnake—to eat (against NPS regulations). He found none. (In fact, both of us searched for rattlesnake in likely places from Bass to Hermit, but saw no trace.) There were signs of recent, substantial flooding in Ruby.

Our campsite along a ledge at Ruby.

Ruby Canyon, a true jewel of the Grand Canyon.

We pitched our tents on spacious flats about 15 feet above the creekbed, 100 yards upstream from the trail crossing. Again, a noodle mix (like Alfredo tonight) works well for supper—one package per person. I use extra virgin olive oil (carried in a 4 ounce Nalgene bottle) in place of margarine in all our food. The pudding mixes don't seem to set with the heavily mineralized water, but pistachio juice was mighty good.

In all of the creeks between Bass and Boucher, we noticed considerable mineral content, witnessed by evaporative crystallization of minerals on creekbed rocks. Its taste was acceptable, and it did not seem to cause any bowel symptoms or loose stools.

> *[Hiking up] Ruby would have been a good side trip, and you would have had no problem getting [down] to the River there. The routes to the River in Turquoise and Sapphire are more difficult than what you experienced in Slate, and certainly less visually-inspiring.*
>
> Jim Ohlman's comments on Ruby
> (personal correspondence 11/97)

Micah in the kitchen at Ruby.

Day 4: Thursday 11/6/97

Micah and Bob below Shaler Plateau.

The weather continues to be absolutely perfect. Temperatures at night dip to the low 40s, then rise to the high 60s during the day. On previous backpacking trips, my body begins to cruise by day four. Despite preparations that included 200 push-ups a day, 200 sit-ups a day, 1.5 miles walking each evening, and 1.5 to 2.0 miles swimming twice a week, my half-century of wear and tear seemed to be catching up. While day four felt better than any of the previous days of hiking, I continued to struggle on the uphills and wince on the downhills.

Reluctantly, we left Ruby, a true jewel of the Grand Canyon. Our destination was Turquoise, after Jade and Jasper. Jade is a nothing canyon. The descent down the western side of the drainage is minimal compared to that shown on the 7.5 minute quad. The only way to be certain it wasn't just a side nook off the river was the pointy hill between Jade and Jasper. Both Jade and Jasper were dry. Jade does have a definite Redwall bay. Jasper is a real canyon.

Landmarks across the river are not easy to distinguish. Scorpion Ridge is nondescript, when viewed from the Tonto here. It is interesting that while the new 7.5 minute quad is quite helpful in seeing local detail in relation to the trail, a 15 minute quad (or in my case, a section sliced from the big Grand Canyon map) is necessary to triangulate your own position by sighting distant landmarks with a compass. This is particularly true when local landmarks are not distinct enough to confirm your location.

Turquoise is a long-long canyon. It does not exhibit the magical aura of Ruby, but it is definitely longer.

Maidenhair fern at Turquoise, a sure indication of perennial water.

Micah walking down Turquoise for water.

We found a slight flow of water from a spring 30 yards above the trail crossing of the main drainage. I photographed maidenhair fern there. Four hundred yards downstream is another spring with heavier flow and plunge pools. I stripped and took a **COLD** bath. I could only tolerate standing in water up to my knees while sloshing the frigid water over one body part at a time. Micah elected to soak only his battered feet in the creek.

After supper, we packed up our kitchen. We would skip breakfast in the morning, in order to get a jump on our longest hiking day tomorrow—12 canyon miles to Slate. We went to sleep early.

Frigid plunge pool 400 yards below the trail.

Day 5: Friday 11/7/97

We awoke when the stars began to fade. Throughout the hike, only the signs of nature, the signs of the Canyon, offered any indication of time. Neither of us carried a watch. We skipped breakfast and began hoofing the twelve miles toward Slate. Sapphire was quite cold, and a very rocky path. Agate is broad and deceptively large (wide). We ate lunch under a huge slab of Tapeats. Its underside looked like fossil worm city. The eastern side of Agate has more side drainages to walk around than at first meets the eye. Water flowed in Agate.

Micah's lunch at Agate.

The Tonto was hot today—up to about 85 degrees. From the eastern mouth of Agate, we could see across Agate to its western side, where a silvery object, suggestive of a 10 to 20 foot long canoe, glistened in the sunlight atop the Tapeats, just above the inner gorge. Two hours earlier, we had come within a hundred yards of the silver object, but had not seen it from above. Now we could only guess what it might be.

Micah above the inner gorge at Agate.

The section of Tonto between Turquoise and Slate is a distinctly fast segment of trail. I also noticed that finally, on day five, I was cruising! We arrived at the crossing of Slate with about two and a half hours of daylight left. Water flowed above the trail crossing as well as several places below. We decided to hike to Crystal Rapids, at the mouth of Slate. It is a tediously long boulder hop. At the sharp westward meander of the creek, a fall blocks the descent. The bypass is up a saddle on the east, on which stands an isolated tower of Tapeats. The 100 foot climb from up-creek is directly up a tilted rock outcrop. The path is cairned. The

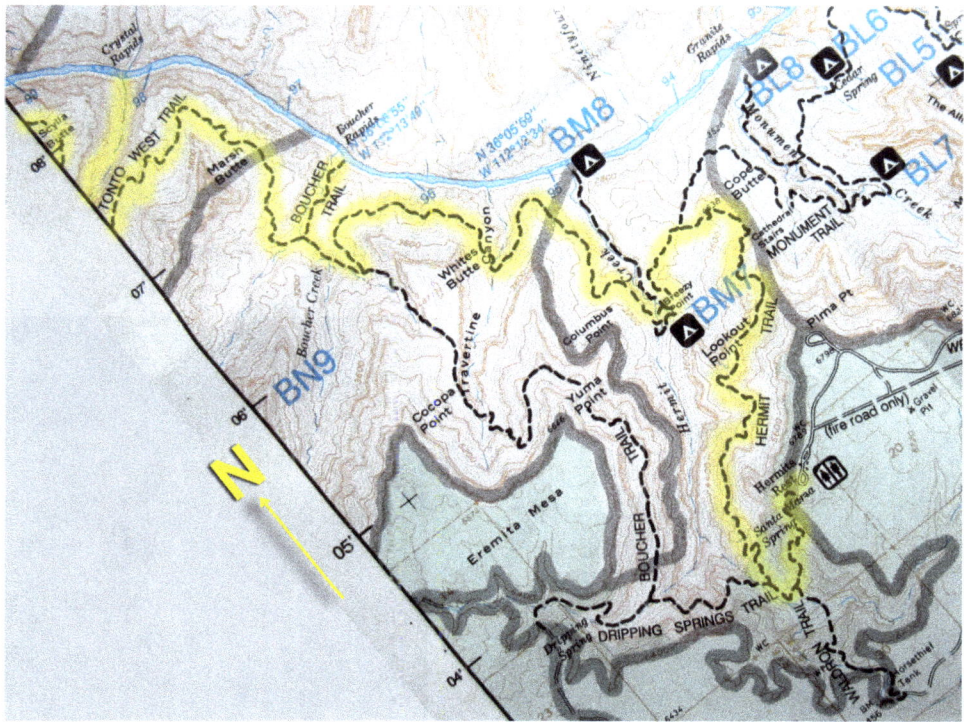

northern (down-creek) slope of this saddle is a dangerously steep, crumbly 200 foot climb, again marked by cairns. It is possible to reach the saddle directly from the Tonto east of Slate, but this shortcut appeared, both from below and (the following day) above, to be a strenuous, steep climb not to be undertaken with a backpack.

The hike from the saddle to the rapids is a long boulder hop, but it and the ridiculous saddle climb are not without their reward. Crystal Rapids is frightening. Monster standing waves and troughs contrast with vicious eddies. If I were in a boat, I think I'd walk around. The Vishnu in Slate, above the river, is covered with a fine lace of mineral deposits left by evaporation of seepage from fracture lines.

Since we walked down to Crystal Rapids without food or water or a light, we had to hurry back before the sun set. I was so fatigued after the long day's hike and the hike/climb down to the river, that I could scarcely climb back up the saddle bypass. On reaching the campsite, I was instantly revived by a quart of water and a pile of trail mix.

Micah passes a small rock cairn along the Tonto.

Chicken Noodles with dried Morel Mushrooms and vanilla pudding comprised supper. Even heated mud would have tasted good tonight. Our tents were pitched on sandstone flats just above the creekbed.

Bypass of the falls in Slate as seen from above west.

The sky looked and felt like the South Rim might be getting some cold—possible snow. Ice halos encircle a half moon.

During the night the wind became gusty enough that I was compelled to fully anchor my tent. Since we were usually camping on rock slabs, I believe a free-standing tent is the only practical tent to carry within the canyon. On most nights, my Eureka Timberlite

Micah at Crystal Rapids.

Micah straddles Slate Creek.

Micah climbs back up the falls bypass in Slate.

was not anchored to the ground in any way. That allows the two side pull-outs to flap if the wind picks up, and it causes the tent to look sloppy, but it sheds water well that way. On nights like tonight, when the wind picks up, I use the hook of an aluminum tent pin to grasp a normally staked part of the tent. Then I trap the tent pin beneath a rock that is heavy enough to keep the pin immobilized. Tonight I also added a guy rope to the apex at the front and back.

> *In Slate you could have hiked around the big meander, instead of climbing up and over the saddle to the east. The first fall in the meander is easily bypassed; the following pool requires a quick run-around (using centrifugal force and relying on good friction); the final big fall can be gingerly downclimbed to the right (facing downcanyon). There are also two "scrambler's specials" into lower Slate, both of which drop off the Tonto on the east side of Slate. You probably also know that one can ascend Slate Canyon, clear to the Rim at Jicarilla Point. This is a very interesting, and worthwhile trip in itself, and a loop can be made out of dropping off the Rim into Slate and then returning via the Boucher and upper Dripping Springs Trails. Since the Boundary Line road is now closed to vehicles, one needs to access Jicarilla via Homestead Tank, and some might consider tedious the 5-6 mile walk back on the Rim. An alternate idea would be to use two vehicles: one at Homestead and one at Hermit's Rest; although this would spoil the loop aspect of the trip.*
>
> Jim Ohlman Comments on Slate
> (personal correspondence 11/97)

Day 6: Saturday 11/8/97

Barrel cactus in Slate Canyon.

This morning, we took our sweet time getting packed. It seemed to take forever to hike beyond the Slate drainage. The trail is rocky and steep on the eastern side. There is a beautiful view up river about midway to Topaz/Boucher. A view of the Redwall slope of Boucher Trail is impressive. The descent down the western side of the Topaz drainage is very steep, rocky, loose and long. Micah took a skid. Only scratches and bruises.

While he soothed his wounds at the junction of Topaz and Boucher, I walked without pack up to see Louis Boucher's homestead. I found some lovely green grass above the Boucher Trail junction. Also, I located a few stone foundations for small buildings. It's hard to tell much about what was once there. He picked a pretty spot, but what he built and what he planted are no longer discernible from the remnants.

East of Slate mouth, looking west.

Though Topaz is dry as far as I could see, water flows briskly in Boucher. The hike down the usually broad bed to the river is long, uncomfortable and tiresome, over sand, pebbles, boulders and occasional, short falls. Boucher Rapids appears more survivable than Crystal. We watched four inflatable 2-man dories slosh their way through. Passengers and crew were bundled up like skiers at Copper Mountain. Micah and I stood in clothing appropriate to the 75 degree temperature on the beach. The sky, which had been cloudless all day, darkened with heavy clouds near dusk.

Approaching Boucher from the west.

We pitched our tents on the sandy beach about ten feet above river level. After supper, and just before dark, I discovered a middle-age couple straggling in from up the creek. They said that they began the Redwall descent of Boucher Trail at 1 p.m. These were the first people we had spoken with since the top of the Redwall at Bass.

Louis Boucher's stone foundation in Boucher Canyon.

Today I had noticed that whoever or whatever preceded us along the Tonto apparently played golf with any prickly pear alongside the trail. While it's hard to imagine some animal knocking the cacti about, it is equally difficult to imagine a human backpacker expending the energy required to swat at so many cacti over so long a distance. Who knows?

Helicopters have been soaring back and forth to the North Rim all day long, two at a time. Either a major SAR mission, or a lot of tourists with more money than they know what to do with. There is something deeply frustrating about hiking in an area so remote that we encounter no other people, and yet have our solitude disrupted ten to twenty times a day by a helicopter whose only purpose is to make it painless for others to "see" the Canyon. Sigh!

Micah at juncture of Topaz and Boucher Creeks.

At Boucher beach, I found a huge collection of driftwood in every imaginable shape, just below the rapids, in what was probably a massive eddy during the high water several days ago. My favorite was a large cactus skeleton about 4 feet long and 8 inches wide.

Day 7: Sunday 11/9/97

After a balmy night at Boucher Rapids, the hike up from the river was not quite as tedious as the hike down. We met 3 men who had camped near the Boucher homestead. One said he had thought several times about hiking from Bass. I mentioned the fortuitous combination of dry road to Pasture Wash and wet canyons.

Micah soothes his feet in the Boucher beach sand.

Micah and I lost the Boucher Trail as it climbed from the main creekbed. We bushwhacked up the eastern drainage (difficult going) until we sighted a small cairn about sixty feet above us to the north of the side drainage. Once we regained the trail, it was only a short way to the pagoda-sized (tourist variety) cairn marking the junction of Boucher Trail with Tonto East. Most of the Tonto Trail between Boucher and Hermit is steep, crumbly, difficult walking, rewarded by many truly spectacular views up and down the river. Both the difficulty and the views are the result of how narrow the Tonto Platform becomes and how close to the edge of the Tapeats cliff the trail must pass. Despite the preceding, there is seldom any sense of exposure.

Pagoda-size cairn above eastern Boucher Canyon.

Inner gorge east of Boucher beach.

I remember water flowing in Travertine, but both Micah's recollection and my photo at the trail crossing say that Travertine was dry. So I'm not really sure whether or not Travertine was dry when we visited. The steep descent and ascent of Travertine offers unusual views of the massive travertine deposits, which appear to be

Bull snake along Tonto west of Travertine.

colossal mounds of frozen mud. While there is supposed to be a "fairly easy route" down Travertine to the river, I was unable to find a reasonable route to the bed of Travertine. From the trail crossing of the drainage, the creek cascades down a precipitous and jagged, 100-foot travertine waterfall.

Views of Hermit Trail and Hermit Canyon are wonderful when approaching from Tonto West. I was depressed to sight the half-mile long switchback up the Muav of Hermit Trail, tomorrow's prelude to the Cathedral Stairs. Within Hermit Canyon below, the stone walls of the constructed trail to the rapids hug the Tapeats cliff. It was hard to believe that Micah and I had hiked down that trail from Hermit Creek campsite to the rapids and back to Hermit Creek, both in total darkness and with only enough battery power to occasionally search for cairns. We had relied on the touch of our walking sticks, like blind men. That had

Pie crust Tapeats above the inner gorge west of Travertine.

been over Christmas of 1991. Now, we both carried those very same walking sticks. The sight of the steep trail, tenuously clinging to the cliff below, sent chills up my spine.

Micah took the high campsite at Hermit Creek—the one with a shade tree and a flat-top boulder—also the one nearest the latrine. To my surprise, I never smelled the latrine during our stay. The half moon glowed brilliantly through billows of clouds above the eastern Supai cliff. Micah and I discussed the possibility of hiking out by walking up the Hermit drainage. It looks shorter, going straight up to Dripping Springs Trail, but we both agreed that it

Travertine Canyon.

might take longer, since the straight shot up the Redwall looked steeper on the map than that of the Boucher. We decided to wimp our way up Hermit Trail.

Looking down on Hermit Camp from the west.

Hermit Creek campsite was home to about a dozen folks tonight. From the western cliff, I had seen another three or four tents down at the river.

Since the NPS' metal hanging bar was overpopulated with backpacks, their straps dangling temptingly near the ground, Micah and I decided to rig our own defenses against the varmints. We suspended both our food bags from a rope line drawn between the shade tree and the corner of the boulder. Strategic clothespins (I always carry 2 or 3) make the rope traverse a little more challenging for the more persistent critters. Many mice scampered through the fractures in the boulder, on which we prepared and ate our supper, then suddenly reversed their course upon realizing that they were about to collide with a seated human. This was our cloudiest night so far.

We agreed to skip breakfast in the morning in order to start the climbout early. We had consumed the contents of two large Sigg fuel bottles and about 1½ candles in my UCO candle lantern.

It was odd to hear jolly conversations nearby.

Our tents at Hermit Camp.

Looking up Hermit Canyon.

Day 8: Monday 11/10/97 - Climbout

We awoke at first light. No breakfast today. We packed and started climbing. I don't remember the trail from Hermit Camp up onto the Tonto being quite so steep. There were signs of recent mules corralled in the foundations of the old Hermit Camp kitchen. Two hikers emerged from the Hermit Camp area (they had apparently taken a wrong turn here earlier) and resumed their climb out. Passing the trail junction to Hermit Rapids reminded me of the effort I spent trying to recreate the experience of our 1991 night hike into the inner gorge within the pages of my never published novel, Canyon Game, written as a first draft in 1993.

At the junction with Tonto East, Micah and I separated to hike our own hikes to the rim. I was sorely tempted to continue on the Tonto to the saddle below Cope Butte to look into Monument again. I climbed Hermit instead, eventually ascending the Muav on what I call the "world's longest switchback."

I followed the course of those above me, as they vanished into the base of the Redwall. Cathedral Stairs lie ahead, but I could not really recall their appearance. On seeing it again, after six years, I still didn't remember having seen it before. Improbably steep switchbacks of tortured, broken trail climbed in fits of profound exertion. As I rose, "one step at a time," step by step, breath by breath, the eastern view of the

Flagstone switchback of the Hermit Trail.

Canyon opened. Part way up the Redwall, I heard the jubilant "Tarzan" yell of a hiker who had just reached the top of the Redwall.

I did recall that three or four miles of undulating Supai lay between the stairs and Santa Maria Spring, whose name eluded me until I read it on the sign.

I thought I could almost separate Wescogami, Monakacha and Watahomigi on the far side of Hermit. I followed the course of the creek below me, trying to evaluate the difficulty of just walking out of the Canyon up the Hermit drainage. In that regard, the Supai cliffs seemed more of a barrier than the smooth, steep Redwall slope in the creek valley.

Here, on the Hermit Trail, I was reintroduced to the massive rockslides that had obstructed the trail over the decades since the NPS stopped all trail maintenance. House-sized boulders necessitated serpentine climbing routes to regain the trail on the far side. Massive esplanade cliff caps the Supai here, and it was in Esplanade cliff that I once again saw Santa Maria Spring.

Just beyond, a descending, broadly smiling party (Micah later said they "must be religious freaks") told me that they had just seen bighorn sheep grazing across the near valley, on the Supai cliffs. I looked repeatedly as I proceeded, but did not see them. (Micah said at the rim that he saw what looked to him like deer, rather than sheep.)

I walked alone into the crumbled, dusty Hermit shale slope. The nylon rope wrapping and wrist loop of my hand-carved, solid walnut, Marsh-Wheeling Deluxe Stogie walking stick had lost every trace of red from my previous Canyon trips, and had acquired none on this trip. I dipped my hand into the rusted, dry powder at my feet and massaged it into the rope. That should last at least a decade*. From the Hermit shale portion of the trail, the appearance of Dripping Springs Trail seems more inviting than from the pages of a trail guide. I'll have to walk it some day.

The Coconino switchbacks presented the greatest contrast with my recollection of their descent years earlier. Degradation of the cobblestone and erosion of the adjacent soil were more suggestive of the ancient shrines of Rhodes, Greece, than of a trail built less than 100 years ago. Even the intact portions were so steep as to present difficulty walking. I walked slowly and rested often.

All day, the sky, for the first time during this trip, remained overcast, keeping the ambient temperature perfect for climbing in a sleeveless T-shirt. Into the Toroweap, I began to see more descending hikers who, bundled in color-coordinated fleece jackets, hats, gloves, looked quizzically at the rivulets of sweat pouring from my scantily clothed body.

"Sleeveless must be out of style!" I shouted to a comparably sleeveless woman climbing below me.

Micah sat, packless, above the trail. "How far are you from the parking lot?" I asked. "Only about two miles," he replied with enthusiasm. He howled at my response, all non-verbal. Fifty yards later, I stood at the edge of the gravel parking lot.

Improbably contoured cars, painted in improbably brilliant colors rested side by side. I failed to recognized my nearby 1984 Bronco II, which I had owned for 13 years.

One group had chilled Champagne waiting for their members. Micah and I dumped our equipment into the car, lit our victory cigars, and allowed the car to propel us, under its own power, back toward the village, toward the showers and the laundry.

Storm clouds over the Canyon 1997.

*My solid walnut, hand-carved Marsh Wheeling Deluxe Stogie walking staff met its demise a few years later, when I used it to attempt a home-run swing into a raccoon that was latched onto my dog's neck. The raccoon let go, and ran away. The walking stick snapped in half. A broken bat.

Tonto East 98
Tanner—Escalante—Tonto—Bright Angel
December 22-31 1998
Bob, Micah, Richard, Andy, Paulette (10 days)

About the Hike

"Tonto East" was an oversimplification. Something to have embroidered on a hat. For me, *Stogie* (Bob) and my 21 year old son, Micah, this hike was to be the "other half" of the Tonto Trail. (Micah's 21st birthday was a

week after returning from the hike.) He and I had hiked the South Bass-Tonto-Hermit loop the previous year, and had hiked the Hermit-BA loop six years prior. Since I had been planning for a 10 day hike this year, I decided to make it more challenging by throwing in the Tanner and Escalante Route as well. Mercifully, I elected early in the planning to leave off an out-and-back from Tanner Beach, east on the Beamer Trail to the confluence of the Little Colorado. The way things turned out, we had our hands full with just the Tanner and

Escalante. The Escalante is called a "route" instead of a "trail," because there are spots that require serious rock scrambling, a rope for gear, and a bit of courage. No actual rock climbing skills were required.

As the plans fell together, we evolved into a group of 5 (actually 6, but one member had to cancel at the last minute). In addition to Micah and myself, we would be accompanied by my brother, *Raudy* (Richard), who was a seasoned AT hiker, but new to the Canyon, and two friends, Andy and *Xena* (Paulette), both of whom were less experienced hikers. In retrospect, Andy and Xena's hiking skills would have been easily up to hiking a New Hance-Tonto-BA loop. The Escalante Route was right on edge of being doable. Since I had planned this as a hike for myself and Micah, I had not taken their abilities into consideration, and was hesitant to jeopardize the backcountry permit already in hand.

It is worth pointing out that, of our group, Micah was the only one clearly in the flower of youth. Raudy, Andy and I were past the half century mark. Xena, of course, was of an indeterminate, though much younger age than us three old guys.

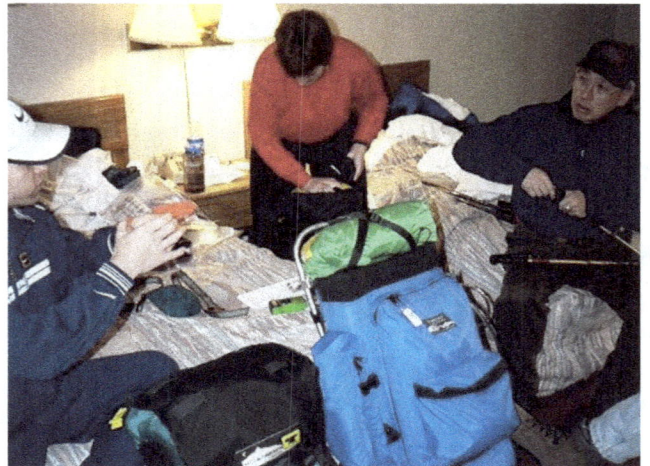

We arrived in Flagstaff two evenings prior to the start of the hike. This gave us a chance to have a nice dinner at a real restaurant (the late, Asian Gourmet), as well as to shop at the local outfitter's in the morning. Our drive to the South Rim was leisurely. The winter dearth of tourists there is always a pleasure.

Day 1: Lipan Point to Tanner Beach [Tanner Trail]

Initially, my thought was to camp at Mather Campground on the South Rim the night before the hike. That's what I had often done. But sanity prevailed. The forecast was for an overnight low of 5° F. Instead, we all shared a room at Maswik Lodge (significantly cheaper in winter than in summer), and fed our faces at their dinner buffet. The following morning, before sunrise, we drove our two cars to the lot at Bright Angel Lodge, left one, with our travel gear in the trunk, and all of us piled into the other car to drive out to Lipan Point, where we would begin our hike. [A "Harvey Car," as they call the taxi service of the Fred Harvey Enterprises concession, would have cost $36 from Maswik to Lipan Point for 1 person, and $12 for each additional person. i.e. $96] We reached Lipan Point just before sunrise. The temperature was 15° F, with 30 mph winds and a clear sky. We left our second car here, to be reclaimed after the hike.

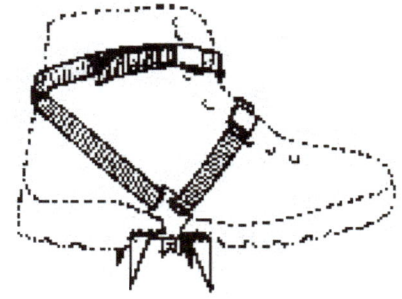

When I look out to the bleak desolation of the Canyon on a bitter winter morning, I can't help but question the arrogance of just hiking on down. What if one of us should slip on the ice and snow of the upper Tanner? What if the "perennial" water sources along the Tonto are dry? What if the narrow slot of Seventyfivemile Canyon is flooding? But I had always just hiked on down.

I knew that there was a good chance upper Tanner Trail would be snow-covered this time of year. For this likelihood, we each carried, and now donned, a pair of ClimbHigh brand instep crampons. These have serious, crossing straps and 4 no-nonsense points that extend over an inch beneath the boot. They list for about $30 a pair. [You may have seen, or even carried, the much milder "ice cleat", that simply straps around the instep of the boot. I used the cheaper ones on the

Micah attaches instep crampons at Lipan Point.

Appalachian Trail in a snow storm. I discovered that the cleat tends to rotate to the side of the boot when any side force is applied. That is to say, it fails to remain in the proper position beneath the boot, no matter how tightly it is strapped. Also, after about two hours of use, the "steel" cleat tips had bent and flattened. This sort of unreliable performance could cost your life on upper Tanner.]

Tanner trailhead is about 30 yards back out the road from the Lipan Point parking lot. It is marked by a large NPS billboard, just off the road. Beyond the sign, the trail is a little vague when snow-covered. It veers down and to the left until reaching the start of the steep switchbacks. It is in this upper 300 vertical feet of the Tanner that instep crampons make the difference between life-threatening and merely tedious.

Xena, Raudy, Andy on upper Tanner Trail.

Micah in the upper Supai of Tanner Canyon.

I expected the snow cover to end after several hundred vertical feet. Instead, we were being treated to an unusually cold December for the Canyon. Snow, in fact, extended all the way to Seventyfivemile saddle, in the Supai! In the snow, our crampons bit into the crunchy surface, enhancing traction. The crampons came off when we began to notice that we were walking on them. Even without the snow and the crampons, upper Tanner Trail is relentlessly steep. Its switchbacks are similar to most Redwall breaks in the popular Rim to River trails south of the river.

As we approached Seventyfivemile saddle, identifiable as the thin ridge between Tanner to the NE and Seventyfivemile Canyon to the W, Micah and Andy headed straight down, while Raudy, Xena and I switchbacked down to the right. The path straight ahead yields a nice view, but requires you to climb down several non-exposed, six or seven foot cliffs, or to backtrack to the switchback descent. The saddle is a beautiful spot, but on this wintry day, a bitter wind whipped through the notch at the saddle. A narrow trail (not very exposed) crosses the saddle, then traverses the Supai ahead, climbing gradually toward Cardenas Butte. Cardenas Butte is where you can look out at how "close" Tanner beach is. No hike of Tanner Trail is complete without the instruction of this illusion. We were all tired, but still in pretty good spirit here, as we pointed to our day's destination, and those of the following days.

Head of Tanner from Seventyfivemile Saddle. [AM]

A few hundred yards short of the spectacular vista on Cardenas Butte, Tanner Trail drops abruptly to the right, into the Redwall break. To the left of this well marked point is a convenient spot to cache water, if you plan to return to the rim by the same route. Finally getting into the Redwall is a psychological relief, but the switchbacks, never exposed, seem anticlimactic after the upper Tanner. Unlike most of the rim-to-river trails south of the river, when you've made it to the bottom of the Redwall in Tanner, you still have a long, tiring hike yet to finish.

Looking down into Tanner from the Supai. [AM]

Raudy, Micah and Xena at the Cardenas Butte Overlook; Palisades of the Desert above right. [AM]

The crumbled Dox formation, which comprises the treadway of lower Tanner, provides fairly good footing, but the last couple of miles seemed to follow a sidehill traverse, a biomechanical stress that turns my knee ligaments to pudding. Eventually this empties into the pebbly bottom of Tanner "Creek." Following this to the river, the unscreened, one-holer composting latrine is off to the right; tent sites are off to both sides. (NPS would like you to keep off the dunes.)

Micah and I were the first to the beach. There, we encountered three other hikers (who were supposed to be at Red Canyon that night). They had hiked down Tanner the previous day. Only one of the three had instep crampons. The others still bore the remnants of terror on their faces at the mention of climbing out. They had been unable to hike on day two, due to overwhelming musculo-skeletal protest, and had decided to return via the Tanner in the morning. There was no mistaking their attitude for enthusiasm.

We went down the beach a ways and pitched our tents, hung our food, and set up the kitchen we share. The sun lowered in the West, heating the rock face across the river from us. The heat radiating from the stone helped to make the cold, clear weather a little friendlier. When Raudy arrived, he suggested that Xena and Andy needed some assistance to make the beach before dark. It's worth noting that this day, December 22, was the winter solstice, the shortest period of daylight of the entire year. So, while Micah continued dinner preparations, Raudy and I headed back up the trail. We met Xena and Andy near where the trail enters the bottom of the drainage. They were moving too slowly to reach the river in daylight. With the surprising surge

Raudy and Xena resting in the Supai; Desert View Tower above. [AM]

of energy provided by even a short period of carrying no load, Raudy took one pack, I took the other, and we beamed our way to the beach. Xena and Andy followed.

I slept well that night. Sleeping near the river in winter keeps the temperatures moderate (usually above freezing), provides a cushy platform for sleeping, and drones the low frequency noise of the rapids. The weather had been clear so far. It would have been even more restful if the BRO had been able to advise me of any anticipated changes in the release rate from Glen Canyon Dam. (As the temperature up top gets lower, the dam releases more water to generate more electricity.) But they knew nothing about it. Nor could they tell me anything about water sources along the way.

Raudy and Andy at Tanner Beach; Stogie's kitchen in the foreground.

Raudy on the Redwall Break of Tanner.

Day 2: Tanner Beach to Escalante Beach [Escalante Route]

When I awoke at first light, the sky was cloudless. I knew we had a tough eight miles to hike before dusk. Micah and I did a quick breakfast (always oatmeal), collected a light load of water (3 liters) and treated it with iodine, then struck our tents and packed up. Raudy, Xena and Andy required another 40 minutes, partly because they had to manually pump water through their filter systems, and partly because Xena and Andy had not yet developed a routine for getting ready to hike each morning. This 40 minutes turned out to be the difference between their making it to Escalante beach or having to camp on a rocky slope, 3/4 mile short of that destination.

The eastern terminus of the Escalante Route (maybe a "route" instead of a trail, because there are so many opportunities to choose the right path) generally follows the contact between the beach and the slope, eventually arriving at Cardenas Creek. This is the last reliable water until Escalante beach. From here, the trail begins to climb to the top of a mesa above a tight curve in the river, which flows around Unkar delta, on

Micah, Xena and Stogie at Cardenas Creek. [AM]

the north of the river. A short way up from Cardenas, a trail branching to the left ascends to an Indian ruin. At the "top" of the mesa, an obvious side trail leads right, to the cliff edge. Where the mesa here is cut to a sheer, 400 foot cliff above the water, it is usually called Unkar Overlook. Looking down to the center of the sandy, Unkar Delta, across from the Overlook, one can see with the unaided eye, the rectangular remnants of

Xena, Raudy and Micah at 400-foot Unkar Overlook.

Stogie and Micah at Unkar Overlook, facing downriver. [AM]

a multi-room, ancient Indian dwelling, described by Colin Fletcher in *The Man Who Walked Through Time*.

Continuing westward and upward from the Overlook, the trail climbs into the "unnamed drainage" east of Escalante. From where you first enter this drainage until you exit its western extreme, the climb is rocky and relentless. From the eastern face, the western face of the drainage appears too steep for a traversing trail. That turns out to be true. The problem is that the trail on the western side traverses and climbs, all the way over the top of the mesa at its northern point. In this area, we sighted a lone California Condor soaring in the updrafts of a nearly cloudless day above the mesa. The much-discussed, Butchart's Notch is a passage over the body of the mesa, instead of walking to its northern point. Among all the notches in the mesa, it is the only one with climbable talus extending all the

Undercut, western face of Unkar Overlook. Raudy and Xena ascend the "unnamed drainage" west of Cardenas.

Raudy ascends the eastern slope of the "unnamed drainage" west of Cardenas.

way to the verge of the notch. Given the extent of my exertion in climbing the "real" trail, I could not imagine expending the time and calories needed to get up to that notch, and down the other side. (The path down from the notch into Escalante appeared to be even steeper, and its talus less stable.)

In Escalante, the trail traverses to where it crosses the main bed, then continues its traverse on the western face, eventually dropping into the bed of Escalante's western branch. There is a small, 15 foot cliff which Micah and I downclimbed. From the bottom, we noticed that it could be bypassed to the right (both ways are cairned). The trail moves down this side drainage. A hundred yards before joining the main bed of Escalante, the bed of the side drainage reaches a 100 foot pouroff, something not to be encountered inattentively in the fading light of day. Back 100 feet from the pouroff is a seep spring in the wall. The spring was flowing. Back 20 feet from the pouroff is a cairned bypass to the left. This leads into the main bed of Escalante and, in a quarter mile or so, to the small beach.

Micah and I reached Escalante beach just before dusk. Again, the weather had been perfect, ranging from the low 30s to the mid 50s. I set up my tent, then climbed back up the trail to guide Raudy, Andy and Xena around the 100 foot pouroff. I knew that the bypass would be difficult to find and difficult to follow in the dark. Part way there, it became too dark to see without a light. (I usually walk at night without a light, but this was an overcast, moonless night in the dark cut of a side canyon at the bottom of the Grand Canyon.) When I need a light by which to hike, I suspend my Uco candle lantern, with reflecting shade, from the wrist loop of my walking staff, holding it low in front of me to illuminate the trail. This proved to be completely inadequate for identifying cairns as I climbed the barely visible trail. Fortunately, Micah had insisted that I carry his 2 cell AA halogen flashlight. Years earlier, I had completely used up the power on an identical light, in a round trip night time excursion from Hermit Campsite to Hermit Rapids. I now hiked by the soft light of my candle lantern, firing

Stogie and his Kelty Tioga pack at the tiny Escalante Beach.

Raudy at the encampment above the pouroff in Escalante. [AM]

up the painfully bright flashlight only to scan for cairns when the trail got fuzzy.

I knew that Raudy, Andy and Xena were a fair bit behind, but I didn't know how far. I climbed back up the side drainage, and the bypass of the 100 foot pouroff, and again into the bed of the side drainage. In the dark, I came upon Raudy filling his water from the seep spring. He said that, as I had expected, they could not locate the bypass in the dark. They made camp on the sloped rock a hundred yards above the pouroff. I left Raudy at the spring and hiked up to their makeshift campsite. Since they were well established here, I suggested that Micah and I wait for them at the beach after breakfast. I returned the way I had come, slipping once on a patch of ice, bruising my butt.

Day 3: Escalante Beach to Red Canyon (Hance Rapids) [Escalante Route]

From the start of planning, day 3 was certain to be the most memorable and challenging segment of the entire trip.

Even though the distance between Escalante beach and Red Canyon (Hance Rapids) is less than 4 miles, it includes the least trail-like sections to be found anywhere along the path from Tanner to Bass. It is also the segment most confusingly described in the various trail logs by other backpackers.

Andy, Raudy and Xena arrived at the beach as Micah and I were packing up. This would have been great timing if it weren't for their need to "pump" more water, a process that added, at least, another half hour.

Climbing Out: Grand Canyon Hikes 1997-2006

Xena passes down her pack to Raudy in lower Escalante. [AM]

[I had not been inclined to use a filter pump because of the pack weight and the recurring, sustained exertion required to propel the water from the source to the container. On this trip, in which we started some days with as much as nine liters each (because of the uncertainty of water sources), I decided that pumping time was the most significant disadvantage to the pump in a desert setting. A further disadvantage when relying on Colorado River water is the typically heavy silt burden. On this trip, fortunately, we never encountered heavily silted river water—a condition which would have increased pump resistance and time, and shortened filter life, by clogging it with silt. Instead, I used Polar Pure crystalline iodine or iodine tablets. While any form of iodine requires time to act, it is time that can be spent on the trail.]

Xena approaches Escalante Beach. [AM]

The trail west from Escalante beach ascends steeply to the top of the inner gorge. As we approached the east mouth of Seventyfivemile Canyon, we could look down and see Neviles Rapids. The trail turns abruptly left to follow the somewhat exposed top edge of Seventyfivemile, a slot canyon. A short distance in, the canyon and trail make an abrupt right hand turn, at the corner of which is an ugly little exposed spot. About 100 yards beyond, the trail along the edge of the canyon is crossed by a line of small stones, indicating that this apparent continuation of the trail is *not* the one to follow. Looking to my right, into Seventyfivemile, I saw a cairn about 15 feet below me. The total descent to the canyon floor here is about 50 feet, and at first appears to be straight down. On closer inspection, however, it is an easily climbable set of ledges. They were, however, steep enough to require us to take off our packs and lower them with rope. One of our photos gives a good perspective on this pouroff. The most exciting aspect of it was to stand at the top and watch the facial expressions of each successive party member as he or she realized that the trail actually did go down the pouroff. Despite some hesitation, everyone made it down with little difficulty.

Neviles Rapids east of the mouth of Seventyfivemile Canyon.

The walls of Seventyfivemile Canyon are composed of swirling colors of Shinumo quartzite, and are nearly vertical. The wading pool described in the GCNP trail description was dry. But this would not be a place to loiter if there were rain somewhere above. (For us, the weather continued its magic.) The canyon opens onto a charming, small beach, at which we stopped for lunch. This would be a pleasant spot to camp.

Micah along the exposed eastern edge of Seventyfivemile Canyon.

To the west, a ramp of stone leads up to a tedious sidehill traverse above the river, eventually descending to the tiny beach at Papago Canyon. Papago ends in a 25 foot pouroff only yards from the river. On the western side of the pouroff is the 50 foot cliff that must be climbed. Reading about this cliff had caused me considerable worry in the months preceding the trip. One experienced canyoneer had even suggested that I carry 100 feet of 4mm static line, in case a member of my party "froze" on the cliff. Well...I had the static line (at the bottom of my pack, where it stayed for the entire trip). But this is a truly easy cliff to climb. As you can see from the photos, it is a stack of easy ledges with no sense of exposure. The only recommendation that I would make is to take off packs when it gets steep (about half way up), and hand them up from ledge to ledge the rest of the way. Raudy thought it looked easy enough to climb with his pack on, but found himself stuck in the one spot he could not negotiate with a pack, unable to easily remove his pack or go back. With a helping hand, he was out of his pack. I don't think I'd want to do this stretch solo.

Raudy, Andy and Xena approaching the right angle turn in the eastern cliff of Seventyfivemile.

From the top of the 50 foot cliff, the cairned trail continues a steep climb. You climb until you can't go up any more. At that point the trail levels off, and opens into the genuinely terrifying stretch of the trail —the rock slide. Initially it appears that one must simply fling oneself 400 feet down the impossibly steep slide. But there is a switchback up at the top that circumvents the steepest, upper segment, and brings you into the chute. Here, every rock seems to be ready to tumble down with the slightest provocation, but one must go straight down, using hands to balance, but not to bear weight. Below the chute, the slope of the trail moderates a bit, and works its way toward the wall to the left. Once there, the trail glides out onto the broad slope of tamarisk, seep willow and acacia that separate the wall from the river. About half of the rock slide, the part that comes up from the river, never needs to be traversed if you keep to the left hand wall when descending.

Micah was the first into the rock slide, but followed a tempting cairn toward the river (right side), so I was the first to the bottom. I doffed my pack, then scrambled through the thorny acacias to find a good vantage from which to photograph the others coming down the slide. Watching someone else move into the chute was more frightening than doing it myself. My secure vantage allowed me the luxury of seeing the entire situation—of seeing just how precarious it is. From some of the photos, you can see that portions of the rock slide appear to be steeper than their natural angle of repose. That is, it looked like nothing was

Raudy lowers a pack to Micah in the surprising pouroff of Seventyfivemile Canyon.

preventing the upper pile of sofa-size rocks from just tumbling down the rest of the way, right onto whoever happened to be in the chute.

The entire pouroff; without the line of small stones across the trail, I would not have seen this cairned descent; it's more surprising than difficult; it just seems like an improbable notch to go down. [AM]

When Andy got down, he admitted that it was the most strenuous thing he had ever done in his life. Micah laboriously worked his way across the house-size boulders at the bottom of the slide and joined us. Andy, Micah and I watched as Raudy, who was next, futilely attempted to assist Xena, last to come down. There is just no way to easily help someone, and no useful way to hand a pack down. Only Xena chose to remove her pack while descending. She tied it to a rope, then allowed it to go down in a sort of controlled tumble to a point beyond the chute. I'm not sure if this was easier than just wearing it, but she said it felt safer than wearing it. Everyone made it down without injury, and with a good war story.

Micah against the quartzite swirls of Seventyfivemile.

I tried to capture on film the sense of instability, of imminent movement, that I felt in the pit of my stomach when descending the rock slide. The feeling was even more pronounced while looking up after completing the descent, watching helplessly as the others crept downward, one by one. None of the photos measure up.

From the bottom of the rock slide, it's an easy, 20 minute boulder hop to the beach at Red Canyon (Hance Rapids). We were tired enough to stop on the beach east of the drainage, upstream from the rapids.

It is a comfortable, small beach. To the other side of the drainage is a vast sand dune and enough space for a jamboree.

Raudy above the bed of Seventyfivemile.

Seen from mouth of Seventyfivemile, the pouroff and cliff of Papago.

Since it was Christmas Eve, I designated a wisp of a seep willow as the Christmas tree, and decorated it with the single, tiny ornament I had carried for just that purpose. It was a ¾" tall apple core carved from a tiny piece of wood (the whole apple would have weighed too much), suspended by a loop of thread. It is the same ornament I had hung on Christmas Eve of 1991 in Monument Canyon.

Micah atop Papago cliff, looking down into the 25-foot pouroff in the bed. The climb up is just off the right of the photo. Access to the bed does not require descending the pouroff.

Andy passes his pack up to Micah at the Papago cliff. Xena is in the foreground. While this can be climbed with pack on, taking it off and passing it from shelf to shelf transforms the cliff into an easy climb.

The most telling view of the 50 foot cliff at Papago. There is a light cairn in the foreground and a silhouette cairn at the top. The "cliff" is actually a series of fairly easy step ledges, and is never really exposed. Notice that Xena walks nearly half way up before needing to remove her pack

A solo hiker climbing in this direction can rope the backpack, climb to the next ledge without it, then hoist it up.

Xena in a tiny climb above Papago cliff. Without a pack, this "cliff" is easy to ascend, though it may appear quite daunting if heading in the opposite direction.

We exchanged gifts (tiny candy canes, and from Xena, tiny stockings filled with tinier candies). Micah had carried a tin of baby smoked oysters, which he shared with toothpicks.

The Rockslide: *I could not capture the outrageously steep and seemingly unstable character of this 400 foot rockslide in a photo. I took this after descending the slide. This is the view you would encounter if you started at Red Canyon and headed east onto the Escalante Route. In center photo, you can just make out a tiny, dark figure descending the scary chute.*

A hiker should never have to negotiate the broad slope of house-size boulders to the left in this photo; staying against the right wall until entering the chute when ascending is the easiest path; if descending, as we did (E to W), heading to the left wall after exiting the chute is the least trying. [AM]

Although the night was in the low 30s, after dinner I spread my Z-Rest pad on a flat boulder, lit up an Arturo Fuente Opus X cigar (a gift from my brother Jonathan) and stared at the stars while I listened to the Colorado rumble over Hance Rapids. Raudy accepted one of the lesser cigars I had carried along. Micah rolled his own tobacco. It was a good moment. The most harrowing part of this trip was now over.

Later, Micah and I wandered in the dark to the drainage, and listened beside the rapids to the power of the river. Only the nearby frothing was visible.

Day 4: Red Canyon (Hance Rapids) to Hance Canyon [Tonto Trail]

Even though clouds moved in to obscure the stars just before I turned in for the night, by morning it was again clear and crisp. I knew that the South Rim must be at record lows, because the temperature at the river had consistently approached the freezing point each night. Since we were climbing up to the Tonto platform today, I expected the night time lows to get into the low 20s for the rest of the trip, barring some change in the weather pattern. But who could argue with another day of clear weather?

At dawn, I promptly removed the decoration from the Christmas tree. Since I had been unable to identify the start of the Tonto Trail in the darkness the previous night, I had a quick breakfast, then packed up and went ahead to locate it. The water at Hance Canyon is seasonal (unless you have the energy to hike up to Miners Spring at the base of the Redwall), so we would each carry 6 liters of water. While I scoped out the trail, those with water filters pumped their 6 liters.

It turns out that there are several cairned trails that might be considered the start of the Tonto. The easiest to *find* is at the western extreme of Red Canyon beach; it heads up the slope at a moderately steep angle. I left my pack at the base of that trail, then

Christmas octopus. Raudy, Xena and Andy pump water from a nylon bag. This was Christmas morning at the beach at Red Canyon (Hance Rapids). Temp was near freezing.

Contouring to the Tonto platform from Red Canyon. [AM]

Raudy in the bed of Mineral Canyon.

walked back to meet the rest of the crowd. As we headed west toward my pack, we encountered a different cairned trail at a gentler angle starting about 300 yards before the western end of the beach. Of course I had to get my pack, so I did the *steeper* of the two.

The climb was steady for about an hour, taking us to the Tonto. Near the end of this climb, we found a huge boulder with a gaping mouth and a stone tongue (large enough to sit on). We named it the Pac-Man rock, and took a photo.

We stopped for lunch at our first crossing of a canyon drainage on the Tonto Trail, Mineral Canyon. It's rocky and crumbly, and was quite dry. In celebration of Christmas, Xena extracted a bottle of bubble soap

Micah and Raudy in the mouth of the "Pac-Man" rock above the mouth of Mineral Canyon.

Xena breaks out a bottle of bubble soap and blows Christmas bubbles in Mineral Canyon.

Horseshoe Mesa (upper left) from below Ayer Point, at the mouth of Mineral.

Looking across the river to Vishnu Temple (Coconino walls) from Hance Canyon.

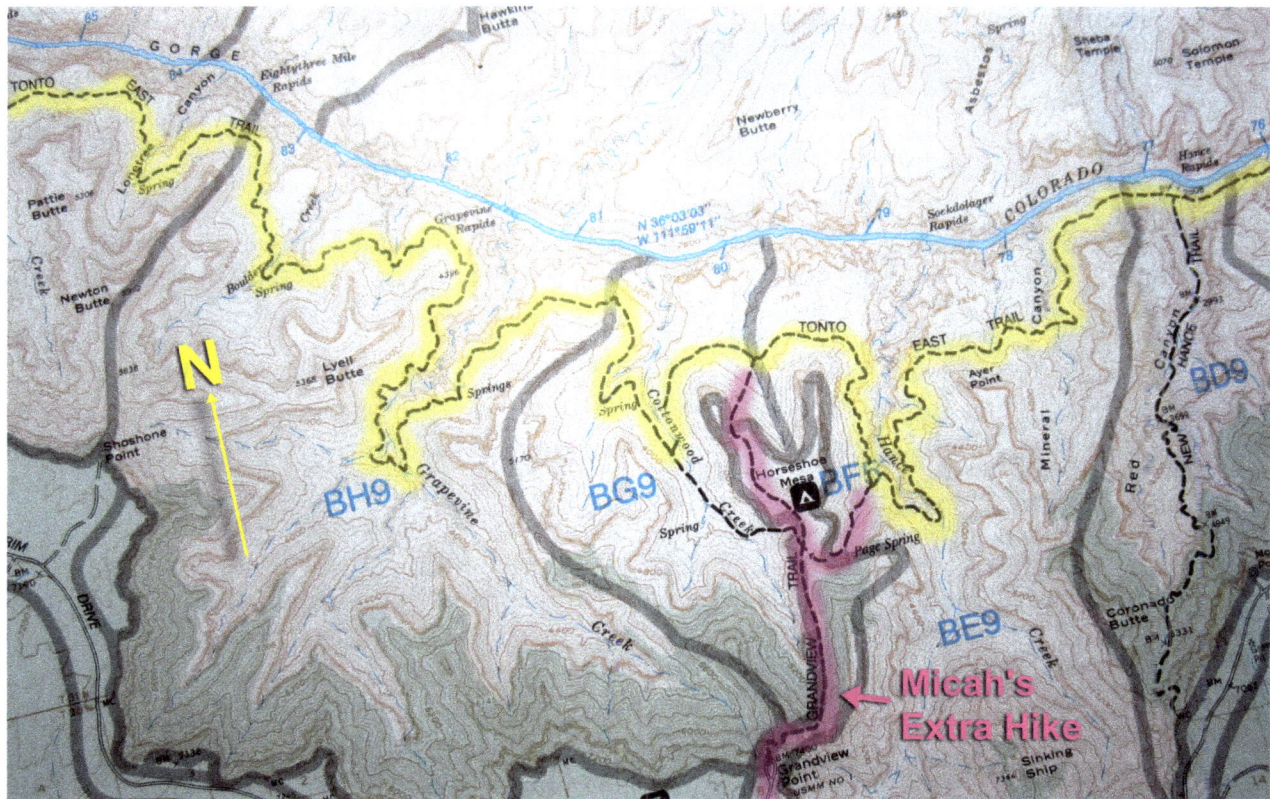

from her pack and blew bubbles. Each other member of the party, except Micah, accepted Xena's offer to blow some Christmas bubbles.

The day was almost warm, despite the chill of the rocks we sat on. Some of us carried personal fanny insulation for such occasions. For a pack-off break, I would get out my Z-Rest pad for a seat. Others used a shower thong (their camp shoe) for a seat. The climb out of the inner gorge stoked the flames fairly well, but sitting on a cold rock will drain that heat away in a hurry. Still, the weather was spectacular.

Hiking along the western face of Mineral Canyon, we sighted, for a second time, a lone California Condor. Six of these nearly extinct birds were released near the Vermilion Cliffs after a captive breeding program. At both sightings, the condor never flapped a wing. It circled from one thermal to another, skirting the edges of the mesas. In the Canyon, where huge things appear to be small, the condor still appears large, holding its vast wingspan absolutely flat against the updraft. At both sightings, I was so excited that I failed to get a photo. The first time, I just forgot to. The second time, I was tardy in pulling out the camera, and missed a perfect shot directly overhead. Then the condor lazily circled into the late morning sun.

Along the eastern side of Hance Canyon, the trail passes close to the edge of the gorge. It's not terribly

Raudy bubbles. [AM]

"Organized crime" is probably the most descriptive assessment of the mouse situation at the campsite in Hance Canyon. These were professionals who knew all the clever backpacker tricks. And brazen... These mice were worse than the Mission Impossible squirrels at the rest houses on the Bright Angel! But still, Hance is a beautiful canyon.

exposed, but it serves as an introduction to some of the more interesting exposures of the next few days. I was relieved to see the reflection of water in the bed of Hance. Even though we had carried enough water for tonight and tomorrow, finding this seasonal water increased the probability that some of the other seasonal water sources might me flowing. It also meant that the perennial water would be at decent flow rates.

Hiking into Hance campsite from the eastern Tonto is almost like landing at a small airport. You pass almost directly overhead, turn away, then descend on final approach. It is a large, somewhat overused camping area. Most of the tent sites are at least a little bit rocky, and penetrating the ground with a tent pin requires the use of a stone hammer. Aside from the soil compaction problem, there are a gazillion mice here. And they are not fooled by easy tricks. Since there are so many mice, there are enough to randomly forage out to the end of every branch of every tree in the area. So just hanging food is not sufficient. The hanging rope needs to be threaded through a tuna can or foil pie pan. (I used the malleable wind screen from my MSR Whisperlite stove.) The mice are also hungry enough to dive into your food bag in plain sight, if you are incautious enough to leave it on the ground for even a few seconds.

When we first arrived at Hance, Andy set up his tent and went to sleep. He had not been feeling well for several days. He would decide in the morning if he would continue the hike, or climb out Grandview Trail. He slept through supper, and had to be awakened and badgered to consume some clear liquids.

It was at Hance Creek that we left a flag flying. I had learned several weeks before our hike that a party of 16 from a Backpacker Magazine interest group would be staying at Hance on Dec. 27, lead by an Escalante Route addict named Ditch. So I had cut the face from a large Tyvek envelope, written a message on it using permanent markers, then attached a segment of cord to it. This I had prepared at home. Tonight, I ceremoniously attached it to a low tree branch near the middle of the campsite. (Ditch, I later learned, recovered the flag and carried it home as a memento of the hike.)

In keeping with our expectations of colder nights on the Tonto, the temperature dropped rapidly at sunset. Each of us shivered his or her way through supper, then sought the warmth of the sleeping bag. Perhaps an overcast sky would have moderated the temperature a bit by reflecting radiant heat from the rocks back into the Canyon, but with a beautiful, cloudless sky, there was nothing to stop the Canyon's radiant heat (microwaves) from beaming straight out to the nearest galaxy. That was the first of several cold nights for me. Since the mean low temperature in December is in the mid 30s inside the Canyon, I had elected to carry a 2.5 pound down bag, rated at 25°F, instead of my 4.5 pound Hollofil II bag, rated at a toasty 0°F. I figured that I would just add some layers to sleep in if it got really cold. Well, it did, and I did. Loss of heat into the "heat sink" of canyon rock is also a significant problem with down fill. Since one of the advantages of down is its compressibility, the down beneath your body compresses to nearly nothing. So, while a synthetic bag retains a layer of insulation beneath your body, my down bag left me with only the insulation provided by my somewhat skimpy Z-Rest pad. (I'm sure a Therm-a-rest pad would have been warmer than the Z-Rest, but, again, I had gone for the lighter weight.)

Day 5: Hance Canyon to Cottonwood Canyon [Tonto Trail]

Prior to this trip, I had discussed with Micah a number of contingency routes and plans, should a member of our party have a problem. Since he was young and immortal, he would be the one to accompany any of the other hikers who might need to climb out early. Then, with that vigor of youth, he would climb back down and resume the hike with the rest of us. We had discussed realistic, alternative routes and rendezvous points. He is a strong, experienced hiker, and skilled with map and compass. He did not flinch when the need arose today.

On awakening, Andy stated that if he didn't feel better by the time we got to the east branch of Grandview (Miners Spring) Trail, he intended to climb out. The truly unfortunate aspect of this is that he had completed the most difficult portion of the trip already. The remainder would be a cakewalk by comparison. The day was clear and cold. When we reached the trail intersection, Andy was certain that he wanted to climb out. So he and Micah headed toward the Redwall break while Xena, Raudy and I continued the hike around Horseshoe Mesa. The plan was that, if they made it to the rim early enough, Micah would turn around and hike down west Grandview, to meet us in Cottonwood. If it got dark, he could either stay on the rim (hopefully in a lodge), or, if partway down, spend the night on Horseshoe Mesa.

Climbing out via Miners Spring, Horseshoe Mesa and Grandview Trail, Micah escorts Andy to the rim. Andy had been ill for several days, and chose to exit before the long stretch between Cottonwood and South Kaibab.

View across the river from Hance Canyon at Vishnu, with Krishna Shrine below it and to the left.

As a parent, I worried about Micah hiking back alone. But more than that, Micah had been with me every step I'd ever taken in the Grand Canyon. This was the first time in the Canyon that I had hiked without him. And our group had been broken. The three of us hiked on with a sense of loss and disappointment.

About mid day, below the eastern arm of Horseshoe Mesa, we wandered a short way off the trail to a high point that rises in the plateau. It's marked 3928 on the big Canyon topographic map. Raudy suggested that I take a panoramic photo, so I stood in the center of hill and snapped photos as I turned 360°.

By mid-afternoon, Raudy, Xena and I had reached the lovely, wooded campsite at the creek crossing in Cottonwood. This is a green, wooded, deep canyon, with a perennial water supply, despite its not being listed as such. The books of both Harvey Butchart and Green and Ohlman say it's perennial, and it appears too verdant to be seasonal. I did not, however, locate maidenhair fern—a sure sign of perennial water, since it dies if the soil dries out.

There was a deep pool below the campsite. Raudy and Xena used it to "bathe" and to rinse their clothes. [Soap or detergent should never be used here.] They spread the wet things over bushes to dry. One item was Raudy's 10 year old pair of bright red Capilene long johns. It looked like a laundry.

I had an early supper, then hiked up Cottonwood to a point from which I could see the Redwall break. I waited for Micah until it was dark enough that I doubted he would attempt the Redwall. Since Grandview Trail circles around the

Looking into Hance Canyon from above Miners Spring. [AM]

Looking into the head of Cottonwood. Grandview trail traverses the high ridge in center photo. Horseshoe Mesa is to the left.

Supai in full view of Cottonwood, I stared into the darkness for a while, trying to see a flashlight moving along the high trail. I saw nothing. On the mile and a half return walk to the campsite, I clarified the cairns leading to the campsite, since there are a number of braided trails, as well as a side trail to the spring. I wasn't sure if Micah might hike down in the morning before I awoke.

That night, I worried and shivered. This was probably the coldest night of the trip, getting down to about 19°F by my tiny thermometer. The crescent moon shone through a clear night sky.

Raudy, in the role of Jiffy-Pop homeless man. [Xena]

This cryptic embroidery design of the custom hat for this trek was simply stolen from the Trails Illustrated topo map for the Tanner Trail usage area. I thought this waxed cotton fabric might be good for hiking in snow, but it does not breath, and feels like a plastic bag, after exertion.

Raudy proudly displays his ten year old Capilenes at Cottonwood Canyon. He washed them that afternoon, then carried them, frozen, the next day.

Day 6: Cottonwood Canyon to Grapevine Canyon [Tonto Trail]

I skipped breakfast and again headed up Cottonwood to watch for Micah. This time the braided trails led me past a small campsite not far from where the trail turns to head up to Horseshoe Mesa. There I discovered a backpack which had been abandoned to the elements and the rodents. It contained a few items of clothing. Nearby were scattered the remains of food packaging, their contents consumed by critters small enough to fit through the chewed, 1 inch openings. To my relief, there were no water containers among the debris. So I assumed that the pack's owner had abandoned it, rather than meeting an untimely end. Nonetheless, I thereafter referred to it as the "dead man's pack."

Micah sits on a "peninsula" at the eastern mouth of Grapevine. Angels Gate is the conical promontory at center-right. The broader Wotans Throne is to its right. Both are capped in cream-colored Coconino.

With no sign of Micah descending the steep Redwall break, I began a leisurely climb of the Muav. Perhaps I would reach the top of the mesa before he descended to there from the rim. (I had guessed by now that he had spent the night on the rim.) Panting at the effort required to get me to the base of the Redwall, I realized that I had brought no water. There would be no Redwall climb for me today. Just then, I resolved a moving speck in the upper Redwall break. Soon, I was able to recognize Micah's orange and white "Snoopy" sock hat, as he zoomed down the trail. Walking back to our Cottonwood campsite, Micah related his tale.

The previous day, Andy had moved slowly...too slowly...up the Redwall from Miners Spring. Micah did his best to speed things up. On reaching Horseshoe Mesa, Micah stashed his pack (to retrieve on his return), and carried Andy's pack for the remainder of the climb out. By the time they had finally reached the rim at Grandview Point, the sun was setting, the bitter wind was howling, and the last of the tourists were getting into their cars to return to the village. Micah and Andy were offered a ride by the last of the tourists, a kind family visiting from India.

Looking upriver into the inner gorge from the western mouth of Cottonwood.

"Snoopy" on the western head of Grapevine, seen from the eastern side. This vantage is the start of a fairly exposed segment of trail into Grapevine.

They were driven to the village (with a window rolled part way down by one of the tourists, to dissipate the odor of two backpackers who had not bathed in five days). Maswik Lodge was full, so they phoned to Bright Angel Lodge and made a reservation. By the time they arrived at Bright Angel Lodge, there were no more rooms. They had called just in time. After a shower (they had access to the travel clothing stored in one of the cars), they went for dinner at the Lodge. Both of them ordered beef stew. Since Andy didn't feel up to eating his, Micah did his duty and ate both orders. After a night's sleep between clean sheets, Micah was driven back to Grandview Point. Packless, he sped down the upper trail to Horseshoe Mesa, reclaimed his unmolested pack, then dropped into the Redwall break to the West. He had just hiked a trail "that'll chew you up, spit you out...". [*Backpacker*, Sep 1999.] In the process of all this, he managed to end up with Andy's extra candy bars, cocoa mix, and a few other items.

When Micah and I arrived at the Cottonwood campsite, Raudy was standing around dressed in a foil "space blanket," causing him to resemble a nearly ready pan of Jiffy-Pop popcorn. Their wet clothing, spread over assorted shrubbery, had not dried. Instead, it was frozen in a variety of agonal poses.

The western mouth of Cottonwood is deeply carved and dramatic, with a sensational view upriver. Just past the mouth, a large cairn marks a trail that precipitously descends to the floor of Cottonwood. I think this is the old continuation of Grandview Trail that connects to the river.

As we approached the mouth of Grapevine, I identified Angels Gate on a promontory across the river. It is a pair of opposing slabs of creamy Coconino. While its appearance changes significantly with your angle of view, once identified, it is an awesome and unmistakable landmark. There really seems to be something spiritual about it.

Plunge pools at the Tonto crossing of the main eastern branch of Grapevine.

We took a long break just into the mouth of Grapevine, so Raudy and Xena could spread out their now-thawed laundry. It was here that we entered the exposed section of trail.

I should comment on the term, "exposed." In this segment of Grapevine, there is a thousand foot drop to the canyon floor within view as you watch the trail in front of you. The parallax evident in the movement of a treadway five feet from your eyes compared to the movement of a canyon floor a thousand feet away is disorienting and disturbing. Is it dangerous? Of course. It is just as dangerous as walking on the asphalt pavement beside the canyon rim near the Visitor Center. If you trip and fall toward the precipice, you're gone. But, unlike the image of shuffling sideways along a six inch wide trail, clinging with your fingertips to the slippery rock above, "exposed" in this part of Grapevine means walking along a typically wide, typically flat segment of Tonto Trail with your brain telling you that you should not be doing this. Raudy and Xena found that, while watching the treadway, turning their gaze more toward the upslope diminished the unpleasant visceral sensation of such a dramatic parallax. It's worth emphasizing, though, that a hiker with an intense fear of heights would find this segment of trail very disturbing. I do not have such a fear, and I found it moderately disturbing.

With all this discussion of "exposure," I must inject a lighter note. From the eastern mouth of Grapevine, one can clearly see, perched at the end of the mesa at the western mouth, the figure of the Peanuts character, Snoopy. No mistaking it. Unfortunately, as you contour into and out of Grapevine, and come up to Snoopy from behind, he looks more like a composting latrine with the lid left up.

About half way into Grapevine, I identified the crumbling talus slope that was the Tapeats break into the pristine reaches of lower Grapevine. It is on the eastern side of the canyon on the northern neck of a "finger" jutting into the gorge.

Looking south into the head of Grapevine.

At the Tonto crossing of the main eastern branch of Grapevine, we found a series of plunge pools with a good flow of water. Nobody jumped in. The weather had continued its magnificent streak of breathtakingly clear days, but the temperatures remained below normal. Looking to the South Rim from western Grapevine, one is treated to a view of practically the whole distance between Shoshone Point and Grandview Point.

One benefit of the plunge pools was a little white noise to sleep by. I went to sleep early, dreading the necessity on the morrow of carrying nine liters of water.

> *I found a nearly uncirculated 1900 Barber Quarter (San Francisco mint) lying fully exposed in the gravel of Grapevine drainage, just above the crossing of the Tonto Trail. The nearest point of the S. Rim is over 2 miles south of this location. My assumption is that, given the coins condition, it was probably lost by a hiker or prospector shortly after 1900. It is now a part of the Grand Canyon Museum Collection.*
>
> Bob

Day 7: Grapevine Canyon to Lonetree Canyon [Tonto Trail]

This morning, we each put up 9 liters of water. The problem is that there is no perennial water supply between Grapevine and Burro Spring in Pipe Canyon. Since the pace I had chosen would not bring us to Burro Spring until mid-day of day 9, we needed to carry water for about three days. In the cold weather, we had been averaging about three liters per person per day. There are seasonal water sources, but the consequence was too great if we took the risk of assuming them to be flowing, and guessed wrong. Besides, by this point, we had consumed six days of food to lighten our packs.

Viewing the South Rim (between Shoshone Point and Grandview Point) from western Grapevine. The eastern Tapeats has a break and steep slope at mid-photo, just above the sunlit, western Tapeats. This break is the route into the pristine reaches of lower Grapevine.

Walking out the west side of Grapevine is long and time consuming, but the views are wonderful. We started early and kept up a moderate pace. About half way out, there is a great view, looking back, of the Tapeats break on the opposite side of Grapevine. Near the western mouth of Grapevine, an island of Tapeats joins the main wall near the Tonto Trail. The view into the inner gorge from this island is unparalleled. The black Vishnu schist in this area bears an unusually high quantity of pink, Zoroaster granite intrusion, giving a sense of torture to the ancient rock. From that same island of Tapeats, we could still see the tower at Desert View silhouetted on the horizon 11 miles to the East. Much closer at hand, the surface of the island is littered with park bench sized slabs of fossils, most dramatically of crinoids (stems of sea lilies) thicker than my thumb. While the island is right out there on the edge, it did not feel as exposed as the eastern slope of Grapevine. Perhaps that is because we could leave our packs at the trail, before venturing out to the island. In terms of stability (of the stone, not of our minds), four of us were out there simultaneously, and lived to tell the tale.

Entering into the eastern side of Boulder Canyon, we encountered a dangerous washout of the trail. The treadway here was narrow to start with, following a contour above a steep slope of fine, crumbly shale. While there was not the shocking parallax of Grapevine, the treadway was narrower, and the potential fall equally fatal. At one point, a water seep had partly eroded the treadway, and then had frozen across the trail. Below was a drop of several hundred feet. Above was a muddy slope too steep to climb. Crossing the ice required tricky foot placement and skillful use of a walking stick. But this far into a multi-day trek, there wasn't much use in griping. This, fortunately, was a one time educational opportunity for our hike. Probably later that afternoon, the sun melted it away.

We stopped for lunch at the Tonto crossing of the bed of Boulder Canyon. Not a drop of water flowed in the dry, sandy creekbed. Instead, in the creekbed we discovered the paw print of a large feline. It was large enough that I placed a quarter (cheerfully donated by and subsequently abandoned by a fellow hiker) beside it and photographed it. Its width measured about 4 inches. It was unquestionably the paw print of a mountain lion, probably made that same morning. I found another, partial feline print, and several tracks of a solitary deer running (I'll bet!) toward the head of Boulder Canyon. This is the first evidence I have ever seen of a mountain lion in the Canyon. I was surprised to find it south of the river. It gives one pause to consider the implications. While a group of hikers must be perceived by the cat as a serious threat, a solitary hiker might just look like lunch.

It was at our lunch break in Boulder that we encountered a young couple hiking east. Cottonwood was their destination for the night. A long way on a short day. They would climb out Grandview the following day. On my questioning them, we learned that water flowed in Lonetree Canyon, our destination for the day. These two friendly folks were, we realized, the first humans we had encountered since leaving Tanner beach on the morning of day 2. (Of course Micah saw and was given a ride by and fed lots of beef stew by other humans, but that doesn't count.) We dumped some of our excess water.

Soon thereafter, we encountered another couple who had started the morning in Cottonwood, and were aiming for Cremation by day's end. Whew! The male hiker had apparently planned the itinerary, and his female companion seemed to derive some satisfaction from my spontaneous expression of shock at the distance they were attempting. While I realize that I'm old and slow, I just can't see the pleasure in a forced march up and down the side drainages of the Tonto.

Huge crinoid fossils on a precarious little "island" at the western mouth of Grapevine.

Looking south, into the head of Boulder Canyon from its eastern mouth.

Mountain lion paw print in the bed of Boulder, at the Tonto crossing. In the enlargement, you may compare its size to the quarter placed beside it. From the scant print evidence, this big cat was running after a mule deer, whose running tracks were over-trodden by those of the lion. This print and its mate are the only evidence I have ever seen in the Canyon of a mountain lion. I was surprised to find them on the south side of the river. I guess from the lion's perspective, a group of hikers is a danger...a solo hiker is not as worrisome.

There has been a lot said and written about the need for route finding skills when hiking on the Tonto. Perhaps these concerns were more applicable in years past, when there were fewer hikers and more feral burros. My experience on the entire length of the Tonto has been that in the few areas where the trail is vague, there's really no mystery about which way you need to go. The river is on one side and the Muav and Redwall on the other. If you mistakenly veer too far to either side, a natural barrier steers you back to the right path. The worst case is being cliffed-out and having to backtrack a hundred yards or so (which I have needed to do only 3 times between Tanner and Bass). I mention this in the context of hiking between Boulder and Lonetree only because this was the only stretch on this trek in which we lost the trail. But even then, we simply followed a reasonable path to where we obviously needed to go, and ended up on the trail again with little exasperation. It's true that walking the Tonto where there is no trail burns up more calories than walking on the trail, since your gait is longer and easier where the path is obvious, no matter how narrow and primitive. But this is not the problem it is often cautioned to be.

Heading into Lonetree. A pair of hikers are near mid photo. This day was the first sighting of hikers outside our own group since leaving Tanner Beach on the morning of day 2.

Sure enough, water flowed vigorously (beneath a sheet of ice thick enough to walk on) in Lonetree. The tentsites near the crossing have a cozy, closed in feeling, though on this night, it was more like closed in the refrigerator. It was a night for jumping into the sleeping bag as soon as supper was done.

From the start of the hike, I had been more confident of finding water at Lonetree than at Boulder, since both Butchart's book and Green and Ohlman's book suggested looking below the Tapeats in Lonetree if the drainage was dry at the Tonto crossing. I was content with not having to do the extra hiking to find out.

Micah takes his turn as cook in Lonetree. Water flowed in the bed of Lonetree, but beneath a coating of ice.

Day 8: Lonetree Canyon to Cremation Canyon [Tonto Trail]

We now carried water for two days, since the spring in the eastern wall of Cremation was almost certainly dry. Our aim was to get to the westernmost part of the Cremation use area. This would leave us a moderately short hike to Indian Garden tomorrow. Today was the eighth day in a row of perfect hiking (and photography) weather.

The stretch of Tonto between Lonetree and Cremation provides, for most of its length, an awe inspiring view of Clear Creek, across the river. I was alone ahead of the others (an uncommon arrangement) when I approached the western mouth of Lonetree. On the slope above me to the west, a herd of about 16 mule deer grazed leisurely on the scant, edible vegetation. When they chose to move on, they walked in a line directly to the face of a six or seven foot cliff. Without breaking stride, one by one, they leapt up the cliff and out of sight. It seemed a remarkably athletic feat, considering the mangy, malnourished appearance of the mule deer that forage near Bright Angel Campground and at Indian Garden. By contrast, these deer that graze unmolested by human intrusion appear thicker, more muscular, and display a healthier coat.

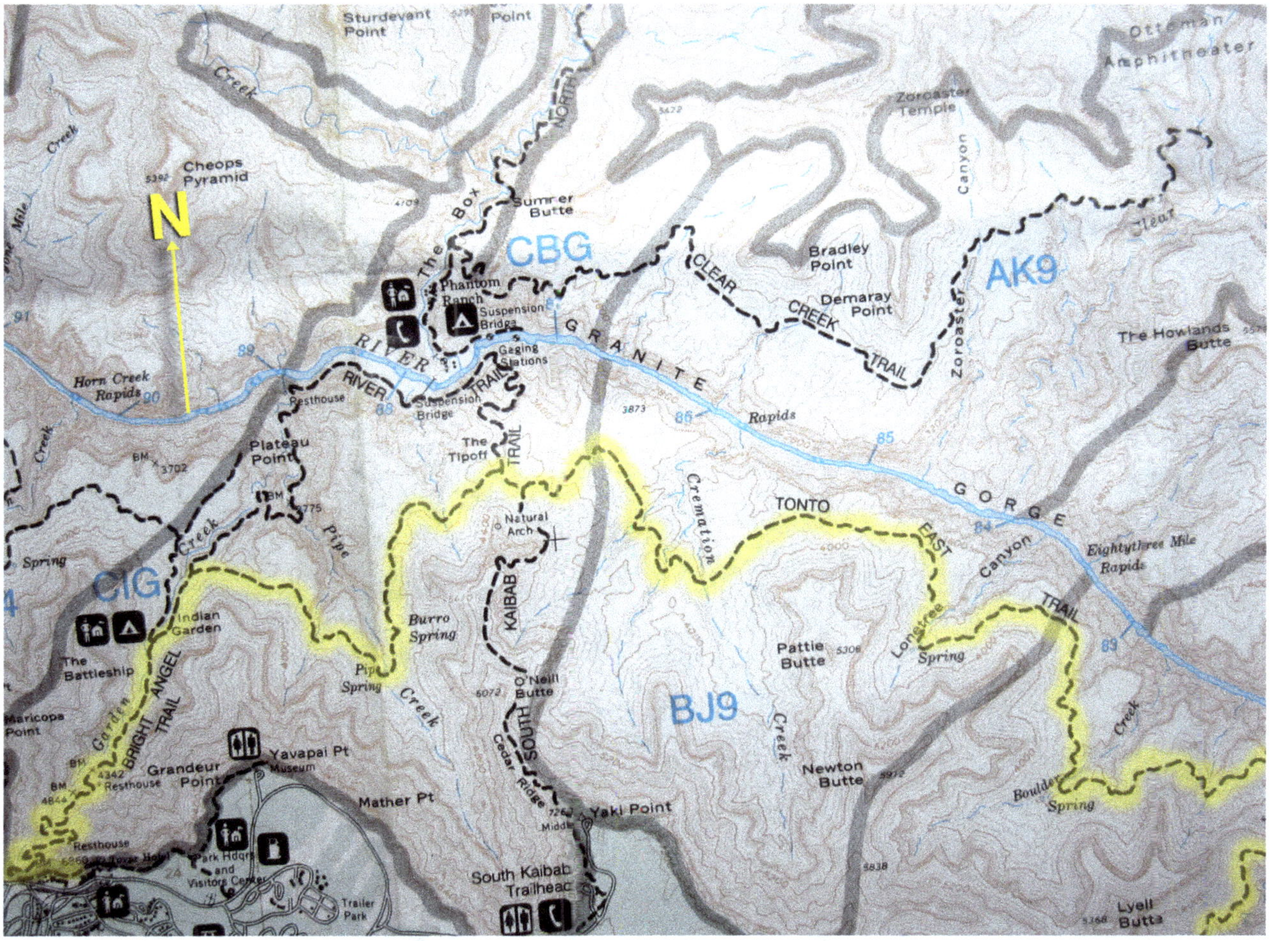

When Micah and I reached the eastern extent of Cremation's eastern drainage, we succumbed to the siren call of a "low" cave in the Redwall. From the trail, it appears as a crescent shaped gash in the low Redwall, with a continuous talus slope leading up to it. Leaving our packs at the trail, he and I began the climb, each of us taking a slightly different route. Raudy and Xena were not yet in sight. We climbed and scrambled and huffed and puffed. Most of the rocks on the slope were the man-eating form of eroded limestone, the kind that makes your hand bleed if you touch it gently. The cave was so much farther away than it had looked from the trail. I was still 50 yards below the cave when Micah reached it.

"It's nothing. It's empty and doesn't go back very far." The disappointment in his voice was all that I needed to reconsider the value of climbing the remaining distance.

Sunrise at the western mouth of Lonetree.

Looking across the river to Clear Creek, which would become the objective of my solo hike in 2001.

A miniature Raudy and Xena passed our tiny packs on the trail below. They waved and kept walking. Micah and I scrambled our way back down, doing our best to avoid serious injury on the razor edged rocks. On the

Dusk over Clear Creek, viewed from the westernmost plateau of Cremation.

way down, we passed a notch with damp greenery. It seemed too small and too far north to be the spring depicted on the topographical maps. No water flowed, but the plants were lush.

Cremation is divided into three substantial drainages, each of which must be climbed into and out of, rather than circumvented. The easternmost was the easiest, and the westernmost the steepest. About mid way through the second drainage, we met a solitary hiker from Texas. He was heading, vaguely, toward the confluence of the Little Colorado. He had some questions about the Escalante Route, and water sources. Contrary to his seasoned appearance, he confessed to carrying canned vegetables in his pack. 'A can a beans can be good."

Late in the day, while climbing out of the third drainage, I noticed dramatic folding and uplift of the Tapeats layers and Vishnu. I was climbing polished Vishnu, looking down onto the Tapeats of the eastern escarpment. This was tedious climbing for the end of a day's hike.

From the westernmost drainage, we dragged our tired bodies toward the large overhanging rock mentioned in many hiker's logs as a great spot to camp. A solitary hiker arrived there from the opposite direction just ahead of us. He graciously offered to share the area, but we declined, since there were four of us. He pointed out an expansive campsite ("big enough for 30 tents") a little further west, but still in the Cremation use area. This lone hiker, whose plan was to wander alone within Cremation for a week, also mentioned that there was a shortcut when crossing Cremation. It is possible, and apparently easier hiking, to descend the first drainage (from either direction), head downstream to the confluence of the branches, then hike back up the third drainage, thereby skipping the "up and down" of the middle drainage.

We trudged on to the larger campsite. It was huge and flat. When approaching it from the West, the cutoff from the Tonto Trail is marked with an oversize cairn. From the cairn the area is about 300 yards north. After dropping our gear, we debated the wisdom of making a run for a beer at the Phantom Ranch canteen. After all, we could see the deep cut of Bright Angel Canyon below us. The vision of a cold beer is a powerful tug after eight days on the trail. We reluctantly conceded that it was not such a good idea.

While I was up in the hills taking care of nature's call,

Herd of mule deer in the foreground (Cremation), with Cheops Pyramid in the rising sunlight beyond.

a herd of mule deer passed across the valley below me. When I was done, I began to slowly creep up closer. The deer became skittish and moved nervously away...

Our Cremation campsite, at the western edge of the use area. Zoroaster Temple on the horizon.

First touch of civilization in 9 days. The solar powered, composting latrine at the Tipoff.

mountain lion tracks at Boulder.

The night was warmer than most of the previous nights. I suspect it was because the area of our campsite was exposed to full sun from dawn till dusk.

This campsite presented something of a problem when it came time to hang our food bag. This was a pure Sonoran zone, with agave, blackbrush, creosote bush, prickly pear, and no trees. To fill the need, I found a dried agave stalk, about 12 feet long. By placing it in the notch of a small bush and weighting the close end with a large rock, I was able to create a cantilevered hanging pole. Speaking of vegetation, I couldn't begin to imagine what the deer were grazing on.

Looking at O'Neil Butte (upper left) from Pipe Canyon.

toward our campsite. The presence of tents and people seemed to be of little concern to the herd. When I finally stood up, the herd relaxed. Apparently they were worried more about something other than humans moving in the rocks above. I recalled the

Intersection of the Tonto East with the South Kaibab Trail. My Tonto East 98 hat rests atop.

Day 9: Cremation Canyon to Indian Garden [Tonto Trail]

Today was to be our day to readjust to crowds of people, something of a strain after the relative solitude we had enjoyed. The sky was gorgeous—our ninth consecutive day of perfect hiking weather. By the time we reached the solar composting latrine at the Tipoff, I was extremely glad that we hadn't gone for the beer the previous evening. It was a little odd to

Micah on what by then seemed like an interstate highway, approaching Indian Garden.

see a packless person inside the Canyon wearing sneakers and carrying a pint bottle of Gatorade. But the Tipoff is a common destination for a day hike down South Kaibab Trail. The park service was even insightful enough to place small trash receptacles inside the stalls of the latrine. The trail here is literally lined with stones on either side. And the rustic "Tonto East" sign seemed so overdeveloped.

We continued west into Pipe Canyon, with its two perennial springs. At our lunch break, we met a chemistry teacher from Minnesota who has hiked in the Canyon over Christmas break for the past 15 years. The one surprise of this stretch was the lushness and vast size of Pipe Canyon. It makes sense when I look at the map, but I always think of it as that tiny piece of

In the overcrowding of Indian Garden, packs suspended from the high tech bars are actually safe from mice and ringtails. Food, however, must be placed in the latched ammo cans provided by the NPS. These massive ammo cans answer George Steck's perennial question of how to win the critter wars.

trail that separates South Kaibab Trail from Bright Angel Trail. Although it is a pretty canyon, the treadway has been worn into long segments of trench by too many hikers. In that regard, it does not give one "a taste" of the Tonto.

Every time I arrive at Indian Garden, I feel like I've appeared at some sort of formal occasion wearing the wrong clothes. Tidy, fresh-smelling people in color-coordinated hiking attire mumble to one another amid sideways glances in my direction. Yes, there are always some legitimate backpackers passing through, but I feel out of place. I become self-conscious of my ripe body odor and dirty fingernails. I do enjoy the ready availability of water, and the comfortable latrine, but the tentsites are jammed together like spaces in a suburban mall parking lot. The giant ammo cans are great for keeping my food safe from critters, but they are needed only because so many people have provided the critters with so much food for so many years.

And the Park Service rangers at Indian Garden are grumpier than elsewhere at the Park. I guess that's because Indian Garden is close enough they get throngs of tourists, but wilderness enough for them to get into trouble. I wandered off to where my cigar would not bother anyone, but an NPS employee felt the need to approach me and remind me not to discard the butt on the ground. For heaven's sake, I'd been carrying my used toilet paper for nine days. I didn't need the reminder.

As you can tell, I don't cope well with the scene at Indian Garden. I'm expecting my wilderness trek to last another day, but I have to return to tourists and traffic at the gates of Indian Garden. Serious backpacking in the Canyon brings out my narcissism. I should really avoid passing through Indian Garden.

One NPS employee I spoke with had lived at Indian Garden for 13 years. He is responsible for maintaining the trans-canyon pipeline. He seemed depressed. Later, I watched as he busted a hiker without a permit.

That night, I heard the whirring purr of ringtails in the campsite at about 3 am. I tried my best to catch them on film, but the noise of my tent unzipping drove them away twice. So I left my camera inside my sleeping bag, and left the tent door unzipped. They never returned. But I got cold!

Day 10: Climbout [Bright Angel Trail]

Climbout is a process that is deeply personal. Each hiker should hike his own hike on the way out. And in a crowded place like the BA trail, there should be no concern about leaving someone behind. Climbout is the time to tie up the emotional loose ends of the hike and say goodbye to the Canyon. I move slowly uphill, so I like to start out early. It's always tempting to (unconsciously) keep up with the young bucks climbing ahead of me, so I have to force myself to go at my natural pace.

Today was the 31st of December. After breakfast, I started out of Indian Garden alone. As I passed the NPS residence, a white-haired Park Service worker snapped an American flag to the halyard and raised it to the top of a rustic mast.

"There've been many times I climbed out in a snow storm on New Years Eve," he called to me. "Doesn't look too bad for today."

The weather (again) looked perfect. "Have a happy new year," I called back. I headed up the trail. That's all I do on Bright Angel when I climb out. Just one step after another. My stamina on climbout serves to remind me why I prefer to hike for at least a week at a time. By the time I'm ready to climb out, I'm in good enough shape to do it comfortably. On a short hike, five days or less, I'm not yet conditioned for the climbout.

In passing, I saved a tourist's life. Two switchbacks before the parking lot, a middle-age woman slipped on the ice as she descended past me. I grabbed her arm and prevented her from sliding off the fifty foot drop. She thanked me, and asked if I would accompany her the rest of the way down. I declined.

Bright Angel Trail within Garden Canyon, from near the top of the Redwall.

Up top, Micah and I found the only warm spot outdoors. This was the bench on the porch of the Bright Angel Lodge. It is an immensely thick slab of wood, painted brown and baked in the mid-day sun. Raudy and Xena had not made the rim yet. After resting a while, I walked to the BRO (or whatever they call that sterile little ticket window place) and reported on the river conditions and water sources along our route. I feel it's important to do this, even though they have never been willing or able to offer me any similar information prior to my hikes. I mentioned the "dead man's pack" in Cottonwood, and the sightings of the Condor and the mountain lion tracks. They don't do sightings. Those should be turned in at the Visitor Center. Sigh...

There was, however, the bright side of civilization. Tonight we would be in Flagstaff, eating dinner again at the Asian Gourmet Restaurant! When Raudy and Xena were up, we rejoined Andy, had a mid afternoon meal at the Bright Angel Restaurant, then headed out to Lipan Point to retrieve the second car. On to Flagstaff.

South Kaibab to Clear Creek Trail, January 2001
Bob solo (5 days)

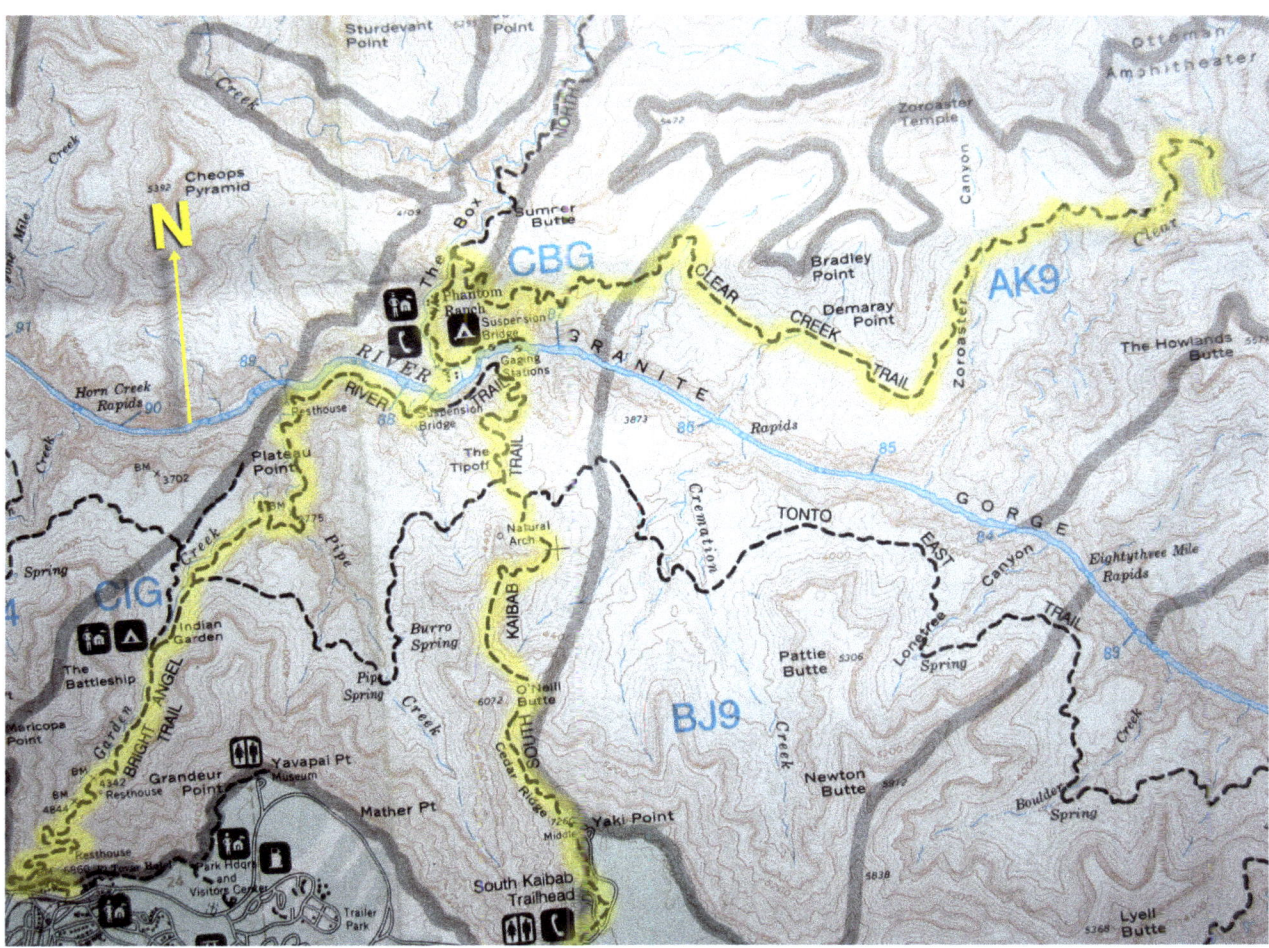

I never documented a contemporaneous hike diary for this solo hike. As I now write this, in the summer of 2019, my recollection of the finer details is imperfect. What stands out clearly in my memory is that this modestly difficult and thoroughly beautiful journey lacked the joy of having been shared with anyone else. Despite the personal satisfaction of going, doing, seeing, what remained has felt hollow for all these years.

For this trek, I drove my quarter-century-old Ford pickup truck, alone, from southwest Virginia to the Grand Canyon and back. The driving was long, lonely and tiring. My body weight had somehow crept up to about 200 pounds, which was clearly overweight for my 5'8" height. But the previous year—Christmas 1999, a planned and highly anticipated Canyon hike had fallen apart late, when everyone who had committed to join me backed out for various—quite understandable reasons, one by one. My backcountry permit for 1999 went unused, hanging as a taunt from a bookcase in my study—Tanner to the Little Colorado and Back. The antidote was to plan a solo hike—this solo hike—for the following winter.

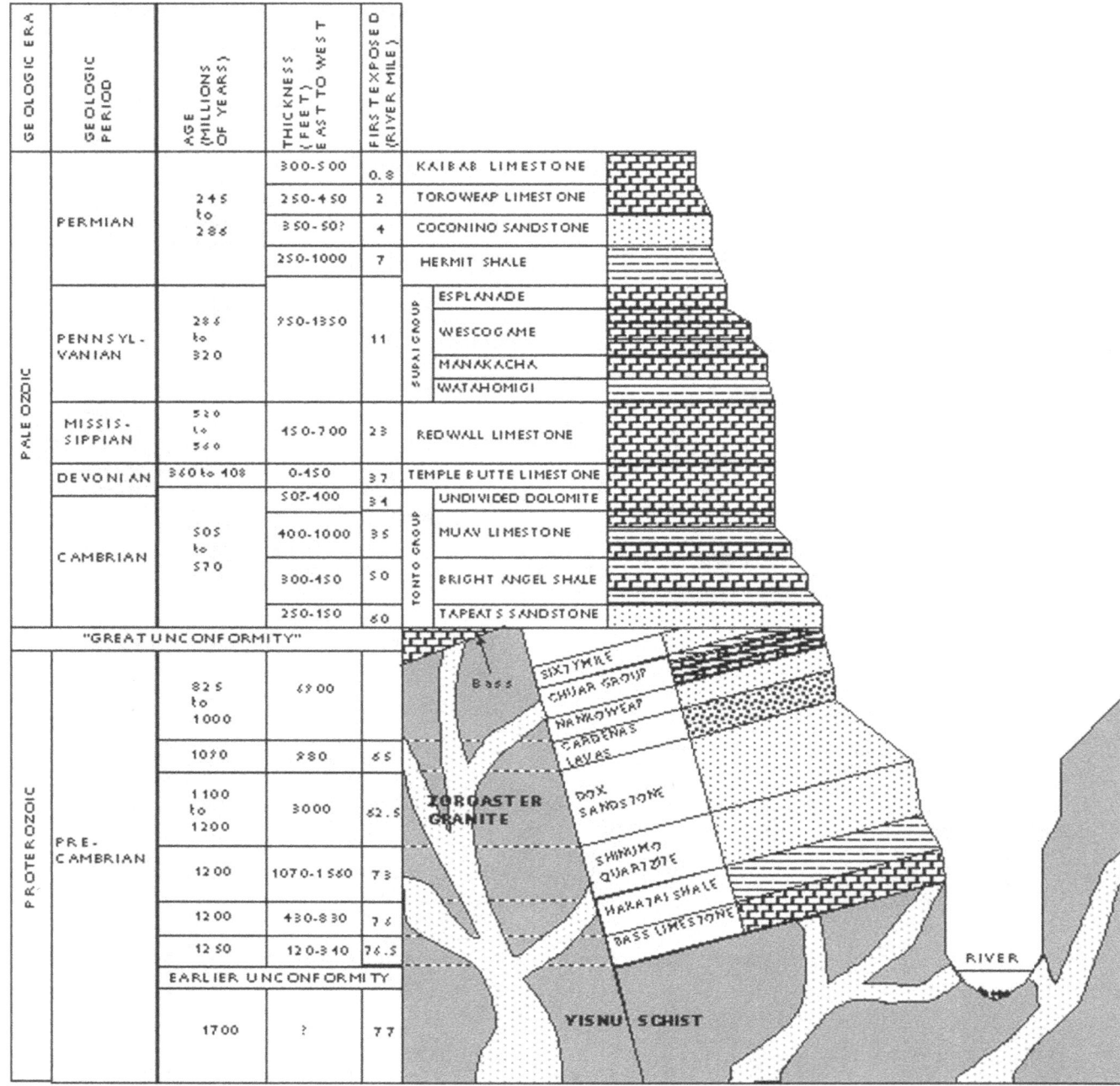

*The always confusing charts of the **rock layers in the Grand Canyon** are useful in describing the unique characteristics of a hiker's immediate surroundings on particular portions of the various trails. Some layers generally erode to abrupt cliffs—like the Redwall, while others usually erode to slopes. The South Kaibab Trail passes through some of the less commonly encountered rock layers of the Canyon, below the Tapeats. This tilted, so called Grand Canyon Super Group consists of truly ancient layers that faulted (tilted crooked), then eroded away almost entirely, before the Tapeats and all the higher layers were deposited on top of them. So, in the lower South Kaibab Trail, below the pie crust of the Tapeats, beyond the "Tipoff", you encounter Dox sandstone and Shinumo quartzite in fairly thick layers, before reaching the black Vishnu schist, with its swirls of pink Zoroaster granite.*

[The graphic shown here is my favorite for clarity, and comes from bobspixels.com. The website belongs to Bob Ribokas, a Massachusetts native, and long-time Grand Canyon backpacker. For decades, he has maintained the most comprehensive website on Grand Canyon backcountry treks.]

Climbing Out: Grand Canyon Hikes 1997-2006

I should be clear. The trail from Phantom Ranch to Clear Creek, and Clear Creek itself are beautiful places to hike within the Grand Canyon. Views of Phantom Ranch from above are dramatic. Clear Creek is remote and isolated, yet close enough to reach in a day's hiking from Phantom. And if I recall correctly, the NPS Backcountry Reservations Office allows only one party at a time within the Clear Creek usage area. As a bonus, it is possible to reserve meals at Phantom Ranch in such a way as to eliminate your carrying 2 breakfasts and 2 dinners for the 5 day hike. (On the downside of this dinner slacking is being seated closely among tidy, well bathed fellow diners on the "return" evening at Phantom. It's one thing to have tourists in the upper reaches of the Bright Angel Trail scrunch their noses as you climb past them, following a strenuous, multi-day trek. It's quite another to be aware that eleven other people seated at your dinner table, not to mention those at the adjacent table, clearly notice that you stink.)

Bob at the south entrance on a frigid, January afternoon.

First morning, first switchback of the South Kaibab trail. Instep crampons were needed.

The Toroweap slope as seen from the South Kaibab Trail.

Having stayed at Maswik Lodge the night before the hike, I left my truck there, and rode the earliest shuttle to Yaki Point. The snow on the ground everywhere, and the continuing light snowfall did not dampen my enthusiasm to finally begin the hike to Clear Creek. Destination for day 1 was Bright Angel Campground.

I strapped my aggressive, instep crampons onto my boots and headed down the familiar South Kaibab Trail, with about 35 pounds on my back. This included 3 quarts of water, held in various-size Platypus water bags—one with a sipping hose attached.

By the time I had made it to the bottom of the Kaibab cliff, the crampons were removed, and packed away. I did not require them for the remainder of the trek.

Redwall break as seen from the South Kaibab Trail.

Each of the times that I've descended the South Kaibab Trail, I have felt fresh and energetic, until partway down the Redwall break. It's steep incline and tight switchbacks always seem to do the trick of reminding me that backpacking downhill (a mile of elevation change) continuously, for an entire day, begs for more physical conditioning than I have allowed myself.

South Kaibab drops below the pie crust Tapeats. Phantom Ranch comes into view.

Reaching the bottom of the Redwall (Ah! I'm already down to the Tonto platform.) is deceptive, in that a huge distance remains to be hiked through the Tapeats switchbacks, and the seemingly endless slopes and cliffs of the Grand Canyon Super Group, before the River can be crossed. The panoramic views change with every switchback, offering occasional glimpses of the fine, black thread down at the river—the Black Bridge—the "almost" endpoint of the day's journey.

The thin pie crust of the Tapeats cliff across the river, atop the Inner Gorge, supports what seems to be a relatively flat Tonto platform on which the Clear Creek Trail passes. Of course, that too is deceptive.

South Kaibab switchbacks beneath the Tapeats.

Dropping into the Tapeats of the South Kaibab Trail never feels particularly exposed, though photographs seem to suggest a frighteningly narrow trail above a precipitous drop. My knees were aching by this point, and my thighs burning. Even in the coldest conditions, the exertion of a prolonged descent has me sweating profusely.

My clothing layers consisted of Thermax long johns, topped with a breathable nylon, windproof layer. My trousers sported zip-off legs, with cuffs that are gusseted with zippers, to allow the legs to be somewhat easily removed over my hefty, Tecnica boots. Half-way between long pant legs and shorts, I can just partially unzip the legs, to allow a gap for ventilation of my thighs.

Beneath my nylon jacket, I also wore a fleece jacket, for better insulation. As my body heats from exertion, the nylon jacket comes off first, eventually followed by the fleece, leaving me in a breathable nylon shirt above the

The Colorado below, and the Grand Canyon Super Group in the foreground.

The South Kaibab Trail over the Dox slope.

Thermax top. The nylon shirt offers roll-up sleeves that can be buttoned above my elbows.

On this particular trek, as I climbed below the massive quartzite cliff of the Shinumo, I encountered two bighorn sheep, standing cautiously on the crumbled shale of the Hakatai layer. Despite their being only about 20 yards above the trail, they did not flee, or display any sense of alarm at my passage below them. While the older bighorn rams sport classic, spirally curved horns, this younger ram showed only extravagantly wide and curved horns. Those of the female were relatively short, and minimally curved, giving it the appearance of a goat.

These two sheep moved only a short distance when an ascending mule train subsequently passed them.

About 20 yards above the South Kaibab Trail, two Bighorn Sheep (a ram in the distance, a female up close) stand along the crumbled slope of Hakatai shale, just below the Shinumo cliff. [This particular sheep photo was subsequently used as the basis for my 2010 GC trek custom-embroidered hat.]

Climbing Out: Grand Canyon Hikes 1997-2006

Time warp: **2010 Bighorn hat** *Unfortunately, the trek had to be canceled a few weeks prior.*

My photo of the female sheep inspired me, years later, to use it as the basis for a hat design for another Canyon trek. The bighorn design was used on both a ballcap and a matching sock hat.

A mule train hauls out mail and trash on the South Kaibab Trail in the Hakatai shale.

South Kaibab Trail winds down into the Vishnu schist. The Black Bridge is seen above the Colorado.

As the Black Bridge gained substance, and the river appeared wider and wider, each new switchback revealed yet more of the serpentine trail to descend. But finally, it was winding through the black, Vishnu schist—the final formation above the river.

What felt good about reaching the southern entrance of the Black Bridge is only that my rubber legs and aching knees were done with downhill for the day. The 440-foot Black Bridge is anchored on that bank of the river directly into a near-vertical wall. So access to the bridge is afforded by a relatively short tunnel through the rock. It was worth pausing in the darkness of the tunnel entrance long enough to allow my eyes to adjust to the low light. Although mule trains don't regularly stop within the tunnel, they will occasionally pause there if a hiker begins to enter the

In this view, the yellow cottonwood trees of Bright Angel Campground (my destination for the day) and Phantom Ranch can be seen to the left, along Bright Angel Creek.

tunnel from the bridge. When mules stop walking, they sometimes poop and urinate. Being able to see the shadowed tunnel floor allowed me to dodge a few road apples.

On crossing the bridge, there is still a half-mile or so

North of the Colorado, the North Kaibab Trail, heads into Bright Angel Campground, with Phantom Ranch just beyond.

to hike, before reaching Bright Angel Campground.

A short bridge crosses Bright Angel Creek, and heads along its western bank, up to the campsites. The

The entrance to the tunnel that leads to the south end of the Black Bridge.

campsites require a permit in advance. With a permit tag dangling visibly from my backpack, I just picked a handy site. (Without a permit tag, a ranger may give you a citation—and a fee, and send you back to the rim.)

During my previous stay at this campground, I used a free-standing tent, and had not given much thought to the matter. On this visit, by contrast, I was using my new Kelty Dart 1 tent. Although its main arch sort of stands on its own, the tent will collapse if not staked-out. At these overused campsites, the soil is so compacted that I found it nearly impossible to place any stakes.

My Kelty Dart 1, single-wall, one-man tent, which is not free-standing, is anchored to rocks, since the soil in the overused tent sites cannot be penetrated by a steel stake without a mallet.

As a solution, I attached the stakes to their various loops and tethers, laid them on the soil, and held them in place with large rocks. That's not ideal, but is adequate.

Another feature of these overused campsites (including all those on the "corridor trails", is that there are *always* little, embedded rocks beneath my tent, no matter where I place it. These can't be removed. While that's hard on a tent floor, it's harder on my back. A Therm-a-rest sleeping pad would solve that (as on previous hikes), but I had chosen to carry my lighter-weight, Z-rest pad, which I've always found comfy when camping on forest duff. It's egg crate foam is indented on both surfaces, and allows tiny rocks to be easily palpable through my 15°F, polyester-fill sleeping bag. A lesson learned—again.

I had reserved an expensive steak dinner at the Phantom Ranch canteen for that evening (a motivation for an early start to day 1), and goaded my legs to carry me the short distance up to Phantom Ranch for dinner. They serve two dinners each night: an earlier steak dinner, and a stew dinner about an hour later.

The North Kaibab Trail heading north from the campsite toward Phantom Ranch. Just right of center, a bridge crosses Bright Angel Creek.

Any overnight at Bright Angel Campground presents an opportunity to reduce pack weight, by eliminating the need to carry dinner for that night, and breakfast for the following morning. In addition to meals, it offers real bathrooms with flush toilets, sinks with running water, and ample drinking water. And, of course, assorted beverages, various souvenirs and their custom, Phantom Ranch t-shirts.

(At the time of this hike, I could purchase the t-shirts only at Phantom Ranch. Now, 18 years later, they are available to anybody on earth, by ordering them over the Internet. Not quite as special.)

Day 2: Phantom Ranch to Clear Creek [N. Kaibab—Clear Creek Trail]

I could hardly move in the morning. My pre-hike lack of physical conditioning was on full display. Every body part hurt. It hurt to get up. It hurt to pack my tent. It hurt to walk up to Phantom canteen for breakfast.

I headed up the North Kaibab Trail. The quarter mile to its intersection with the Clear Creek Trail felt longer, but by the time I had reached it, my joints were not as achy, and my muscles began to cooperate. That first portion of the Clear Creek Trail heads south, and backtracks toward the Colorado, climbing all the while.

There are several vantage points that allowed me to gaze down on the yellow cottonwoods of Phantom Ranch

Signpost at the intersection of the North Kaibab Trail and the Clear Creek Trail (off to the East).

As I slowly climb the eastern slope of Bright Angel Canyon, heading south, yellow cottonwoods of Phantom come into view to the South.

from above. I took my time climbing. The goal is to round south of Sumner Butte, and ride the Tonto platform most of the way to Clear Creek. The flatter stretches on the topo map are never flat in the Grand Canyon. As is typical, the trail rises toward the head

Directly above Phantom Ranch. Sunrise has not yet reached into the valley.

of each side drainage, dips into it for a brief down and up, then slowly descends into the broader portion of the Tonto again. I had learned this on four previous Canyon hikes, but always seem to forget during planning, as I stare at a map.

It was during this hike that I considered the boon of having a hiking companion for commiseration. Overcoming a challenge alongside someone else enhances a personal bond, and contributes to cherished memories. One's impressions of unusual and odd rock formations are enriched by those of a companion. As a solo hiker, the challenges seemed to become just another climb or descent, and the rocks, just more rocks. I was seeing the desiccation and desolation (It is desolate!), instead of the beauty.

What a horrid place for the Anasazi to have chosen as a home. They surely must have been driven into the Canyon by their adversaries. And no one would pursue them into such a desperate fastness.

Ahead, the Clear Creek Trail turns east below Sumner Butte.

Finally up on the Tonto platform, and heading east, I took a long break with a cigar, to cool off from the climb. I've removed my hat, unzipped the legs from my nylon trousers, and rolled up the sleeves of my nylon shirt. The climb is a similar increase in elevation to that of climbing from Phantom Ranch to Indian Garden. In the photo, even lying flat on my back, there's a lot of belly showing.

In the Grand Canyon as well as in other public spaces, I prefer to smoke a cigar only when I'm entirely alone. I enjoy a good cigar too much to risk having it ruined by somebody's complaints. I carried one cigar for each day, even though I ended up smoking only two of them.

The Clear Creek usage area, at the time of this hike, allowed only one permit per night of stay within the area, with a max party size of 6. So with a permit just for me, I had sole possession of the entire Clear Creek Trail and the creek valley itself for this first day out. I also encountered no other hikers during my return to Phantom, until turning onto the North Kaibab Trail. I was entirely alone.

Clear Creek Trail below Zoroaster Temple.

Mouth of Clear Creek.

Backpacking just about anywhere usually would elevate my mood. In retrospect, I was dysphoric for most if not all of this trip. There was no particular precipitating event that I recall. Perhaps it was that I dropped into the Canyon without my son beside me, for the first time. He had accompanied me on my five previous visits, four of which were challenging backpacking treks. I'll never know.

The head of Clear Creek Canyon: Angels Gate is to upper right; Ottoman Amphitheater on the left. A fingernail crescent of moon is above.

Once the mouth of Clear Creek Canyon is clearly visible ahead, there is still a lot of hike remaining, before actually beginning to descend into its valley. Zoroaster Canyon must first be side-traversed and crossed, and Clear Creek's main branch has a separate canyon for its western tributary as well. So, looking at the topo map, all that northward segment of the trail still to hike is nearly as long a distance as what has already been hiked. So near, yet so far to get there.

Vigorous flow of water in upper Clear Creek.

Looking up canyon at Clear Creek.

This is beautiful canyon hiking. The weather for me was perfect. Allowing two hiking days each way might have been a wiser choice on my part. Its 8.4 mile length doesn't tell the tale. The Clear Creek Trail is the only trail that follows the Tonto Platform on the north side of the Colorado. And all the canyons, both big and small, draining from the North Rim are more deeply incised than those dropping from the South Rim.

Camping is "at-large" in most of this usage area, so setting up camp partway to Clear Creek is within the possibilities. The only caveat is that reliable water on this trail can be found only within Clear Creek. A seven-day trek here would have been a better choice for me.

Looking down into Clear Creek. Yellow cottonwood trees can be seen near the center of the photo. That was where I chose to camp for the night.

A layover day within Clear Creek would allow an adequate exploration of its lower reaches. but it's a full day's hike from upper Clear Creek to approach the river and return. I did wander down beyond my chosen tent site in the lovely cottonwood grove shown in the photo. But I was simply too exhausted to go far.

That evening I discovered that, even in the arid Grand Canyon, the maximum ventilation of my single-wall, Kelty Dart 1 tent was not sufficient to prevent the accumulation of puddles of moisture on the floor (and into my sleeping bag and doffed clothing) that had condensed on the walls from my breathing during the night. It's only strength is its light weight.

Day 3: Clear Creek to Phantom Ranch [Clear Creek Trail—N. Kaibab]

Again exhausted in the morning, I had a hasty, instant meal with coffee, and promptly began the long trudge back to Bright Angel Campground. I needed to make it back in time for the "late" beef stew dinner (previously reserved) at Phantom canteen.

The return hike on the Clear Creek Trail felt like a happier journey, I suppose because I knew I was now past the symbolic half-way point. And it would be sort of downhill back to Phantom.

Sights that I had noticed while outbound now seemed more geologically interesting. And the views and vistas more dramatic. Perhaps that was just a benefit of now viewing them in the morning (different

Traversing above the head of Clear Creek's western tributary, beneath Brahma Temple.

Columns have separated from the southeastern finger below Brahma Temple, and appear to be standing men.

sunlight as well as a fresher brain), or maybe even an incrementally improving level of fitness to be out there at all.

I still struggled along the Tonto portion of the trail, but momentum was in my favor dropping down to the North Kaibab Trail once again. I cruised into Bright Angel Campground, selected my tent site, and again pitched my tent using rocks for support.

Dinner at the canteen was timed perfectly for me. And the stew smelled heavenly. Their having just previously served a seating of steak dinner didn't hurt the olfactory delight.

It was during this meal that I became acutely self-conscious of others noticing the aroma of my hike-worn, sweaty body and clothing. I still fret over that memory today, 18 years later. Probably a change of clothes (if I had carried such a thing) might have made a difference, even without a preprandial shower. It's easy enough to dismiss the wrinkled noses of tourists in loafers, as I climb past them in the upper switchbacks of Bright Angel Trail. But this incident lingers in my brain.

Approaching the creek crossing west of Bradley Point.

Day 4: Phantom Ranch to Indian Garden [Bright Angel Trail]

The Silver Bridge at dawn, looking downriver from the mouth of Bright Angel Creek.

I find it curious that I shot more photos during this familiar hike—from Phantom to Indian Garden—than during my return journey on the Clear Creek Trail. Maybe it was the presence of fellow humans that triggered the inspiration, or maybe it was my familiarity with the mundane aspects of this trail segment, encouraging me to look about more. Ah! The psychometrics of picture taking.

I saw the Silver Bridge in a broader context than during my previous crossings of it in 1991. The arc of it. The narrowness of its treadway. Its contrast with the Black Bridge. The "history" of it is that a shorter hiker path from the Bright Angel Trail to Phantom (much shorter than following the River Trail all the way to the Black Bridge, as was previously the case) was planned from the beginning. My suspicion is rather that it was originally planned as a means to allow the trans-canyon water pipeline to cross the river to the South Rim, and that its truly narrow treadway and access slopes were added as an afterthought. But that's just me.

So I found myself observing little things, like how each passing hiker was dressed and equipped, as well as the complex origins of the convoluted geology of the lower Bright Angel Trail. I thought about the fact that Phantom Ranch and the River Trail between the bridges exist as they are today, only because of the Great Depression, and the resulting "Conservation Corp" make-work efforts. They built. They used dynamite to blast trails from sheer rock faces. They made it into an accessible place for hikers from across the world.

A view upriver of both the Silver Bridge (pedestrians only, and the trans-canyon water pipeline) and the Black Bridge (pedestrians and mules)—the only bridges across the Colorado between the Navajo Bridge at Lee's Ferry and Hoover Dam at the Nevada border. A portion of the River Trail can be seen blasted from the southern wall of the inner gorge part-way up from the river. This connected the bottom of the Bright Angel Trail to the Black Bridge, prior to construction of the Silver Bridge. The Tonto platform along the Clear Creek Trail can be seen in sunlight, high above the Black Bridge. The point of Thor Temple rises into the sky above the southern end of the Black Bridge.

One aspect of the Bright Angel Trail that makes it a somewhat easier, though longer hike than the South Kaibab is its more circuitous course in getting from the river to above the Tapeats, and onto the Tonto Platform. So the average grade is slightly less. Of course, there are some very steep grades, like the Devil's Corkscrew, but overall, the river to Indian Garden is just a long, slow climb through a fault line.

Younger folks regularly hike from the river all the way to the rim in one brutal day. I couldn't do that. I need the break of a night's rest, before heading for the Redwall.

One benefit to a layover at Indian Garden is that there is still sufficient daylight to take in the awesome views from Plateau Point, after setting up camp. On this hike, I just didn't have the spare energy to do that.

As with all the other frequently and heavily used campgrounds, Indian Garden experiences intense critter pressure (mostly rodents at this elevation), and requires that the Park Service provide sturdy, latching, metal boxes for each campsite. These effectively keep your food safe, and the wildlife less motivated to invade.

The sandy, lower stretch of Bright Angel Trail.

On the right, Bright Angel Trail rises through Vishnu schist.

Bright Angel Trail in lower Garden Creek.

And the metal hanging posts for hikers' packs reduce, though do not entirely prevent rodent damage to them and intrusion into them.

I've found it a good idea to unzip every zipper on my backpack, prior to hanging it. If a rodent should manage to navigate the tricky hanging post, and gain access to it, at least they won't eat through the fabric or a zipper to get inside. Closer to the rim, at the rest houses along the trail, squirrels will eat through the zipper of an unattended fanny pack within seconds of its being set down.

Maidenhair fern at a seep along Bright Angel Trail.

Another clear benefit of stopping overnight at Indian

Toppled Tapeats cliff along Bright Angel Trail.

Garden is the knowledge of a shorter hiking day. So, instead of a relentless upward climb, a more leisurely pace encourages a more observant attitude toward the treadway and its environs.

Oops! A chunk of Tapeats cliff has broken off, and landed on the rubble slope below. Though it seems like a recent event, that chunk may have fallen hundreds or thousands of years ago, and has not budged since. Because the lower boundary of the Tapeats marks the level of well over a billion years of "missing" layers—thousands of feet of deposits that eroded away over the eons, prior to the formation of the Tapeats strata, that chunk of sedimentary, fossil-filled stone may have dropped backwards to pre-cambrian times, before complex life exploded across the globe.

Bright Angel Trail ascends the Tapeats.

Mule deer eyes in a flashlight at Indian Garden.

When hiking in most non-desert environments, the rock and its structures are well hidden by soil and vegetation. Here in the Canyon, the foundations are laid bare.

I slept fairly well at Indian Garden, awakened only once by the sounds of wildlife moving about the brush. This turned out to be a few mule deer.

Day 5: Climbout from Indian Garden [Bright Angel Trail]

Climbing out to the South Rim from Indian Garden always is an ordeal for me. When I was with a group of Scouts in 1991, they left me in the dust during climbout. I was a mere 43 years old then, and far more fit for the climb.

I arose at first light, broke camp after a quick breakfast and a cup of coffee, then began my slow plod. I was able to hike continuously, up to the base of the Redwall. This is when I began to slowly chant my "Redwall mantra" under my heavy breathing: one...step...at...a...time. I sometimes have to briefly rest at every switchback, sometimes at every other switchback.

While the Redwall is certainly a major physical barrier separating me from the rim, I think its heaviest burden is psychological. My glee is always unbounded upon reaching the top of the Redwall, even though there is still a whole lot of steep trail yet to climb. In my mind, being below the Redwall means I'm still in the Canyon, whereas being above it is just that final leg of the journey, before a late afternoon dinner at the Bright Angel Lodge.

Departing Indian Garden at dawn.

Below the Redwall from Bright Angel Trail, looking north at dawn.

But below it or above it, I am continually thrilled by simply looking back into the Canyon, back to where I've just been living and hiking and laboring. And the frequent pauses at the Redwall switchbacks are scores of opportunities to sit for a moment at the up-canyon side of the trail, and gaze out into the abyss.

On this particular hike, the dazzling and familiar views from the Bright Angel Trail thrilled me more than any portion of my hike out and back the unfamiliar Clear Creek Trail, when my awe meter was malfunctioning. So my memories of that latter trail remain vague, despite viewing my few photos of it. But the climbout garnered more lasting memories.

One of the truly satisfying qualities of the upper Bright Angel Trail is its many views that simultaneously reveal profound stretches of winding, climbing trail—views of where I've just hiked and endured. And of course in winter, that climbout jolts my senses from a dry desert to a world of snow and ice.

Frozen seeps and waterfalls begin to appear along the trail. Then the trail itself becomes snowy. I don't remember needing to put on my instep crampons for the final stretch of this particular hike, but knowing that they are in an accessible pocket of my pack is a winter comfort.

I reached the rim in mid-afternoon. I ate a huge meal. I recovered my old pickup truck from where I had left it, and I headed back to Flagstaff, feeling satisfied, but more exhausted than after previous Canyon hikes. It was an odd, solo trip.

Looking north from the Bright Angel Trail, with snow well below the Coconino.

I decided never to hike in the Canyon solo again. And the Clear Creek Trail would be a worrisome place to manage an accident or injury. While the so-called "corridor" trails may be reasonable for a solo Canyon hiker, having at least one fellow hiker along on a trek in any of the primitive areas seems a wise precaution, as well as a lasting source of shared memories.

South Kaibab to Phantom Ranch December 2006
Bob, Richard, Andy, Paulette, Mike, Adam (4 days)

This hike was carefully planned as what I call a "**codger hike**." That is, even senior citizens in reasonably good health should be able to complete it, or at least die in a beautiful place. The first day, straight down the South Kaibab Trail to Bright Angel Campground at Phantom Ranch is the toughest. But pack weight can approach 20-25 pounds or less!

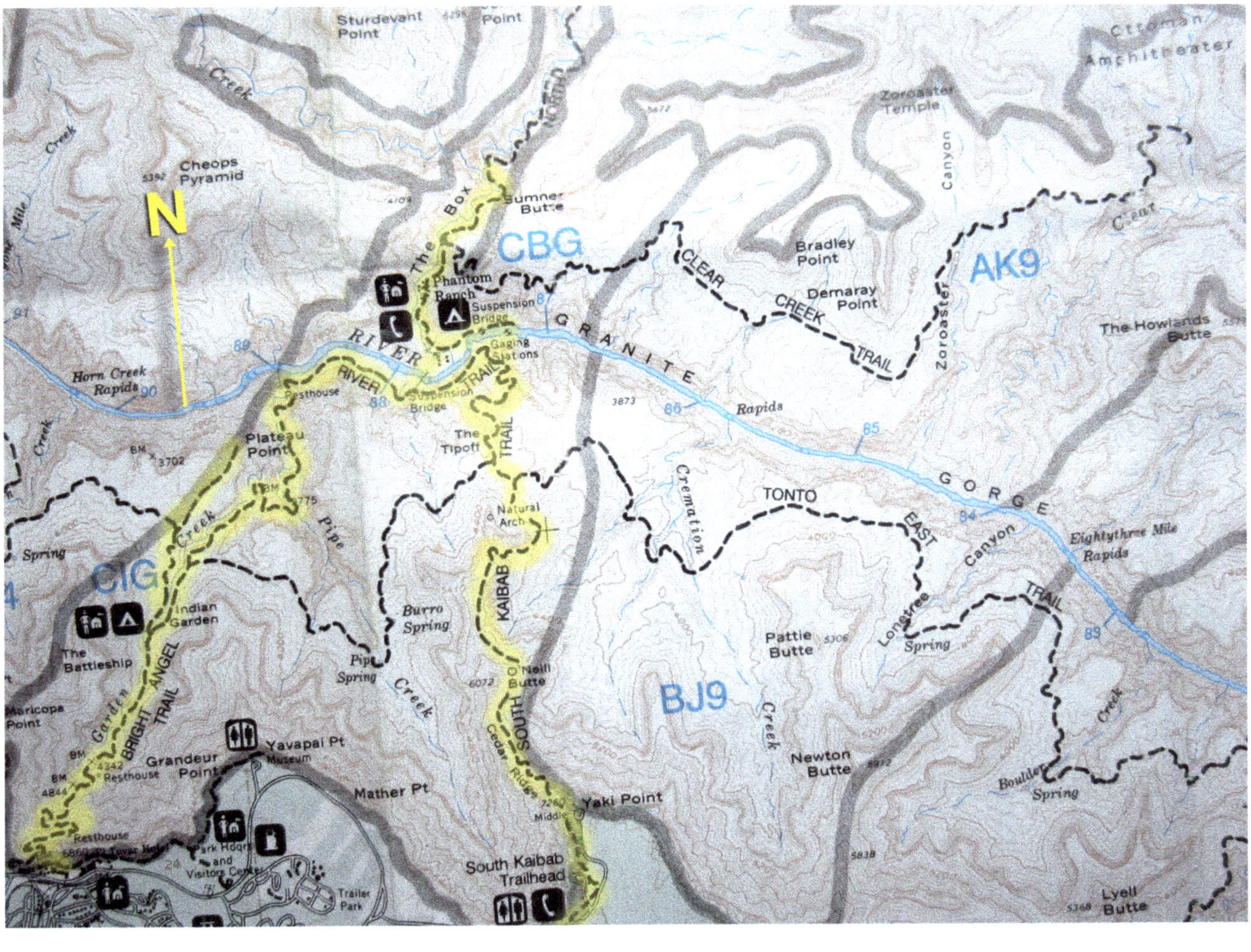

Only the weight of 1 dinner, 1 breakfast, and 2 lunches needed to be carried. So fuel requirements (isobutane in my case) could be met with a partially empty canister. Water weight is merely 1 day's (winter) supply, since there is reliable water available at each overnight.

Travel Day 1: obligatory Krystal hamburgers.
[AM]

I expected aching thighs and knees from a solid day of downhill to Phantom. Then a layover day at the campground, a half-day hike up to Indian Garden, and a "leisurely" climbout the following morning. Four days in all.

Andy, Adam and I began our long drive in southwest Virginia, rotating drivers as needed. We drove straight through to Flagstaff, AZ.

During the early daylight of our second day out, as we crossed from Texas into New Mexico on Interstate-40, we saw a herd of pronghorn antelopes grazing north of the road. Apparently, nobody snapped a photo.

Travel Day 2: breakfast in Santa Rosa, NM, at the Silver Moon Cafe.
[AM]

Time Warp: Their sign in 2019.

Travel Day 2: approaching Flagstaff, AZ.
[AM]

Travel Day 2: Adam, Mike, Xena, Stogie at dinner in Flagstaff.
[AM]

Travel Day 3: Andy, Mike, Xena, Stogie at Starbucks, Flagstaff. [AM]

Travel Day 3: We spent the night before the hike at Maswik Lodge, in GC Village. [AM]

One of my favorite stops was for breakfast that morning in Santa Rosa, NM, at the Siver Moon Cafe.

Flagstaff lay a half-day ahead. There, we checked into a motel, and went for dinner at the Asian Gourmet restaurant. [Sadly, it has since closed.] Mike and Xena joined us in Flagstaff. Raudy would join us later.

The overnight in Flagstaff allowed us to visit an outfitter in the morning, for any last-minute needs. It also provided a much-needed night of sleep in a real bed. After breakfast and quick shopping, we headed up to the Grand Canyon.

Day 1: South Rim to Phantom Ranch [South Kaibab Trail]

Raudy walks to the Backcountry Office. [RCAG]

My usual choice for South Rim accommodations during the winter is Maswik Lodge. During that season, the rates are low, and they provide an adequate room, and have a rather nice buffet restaurant and gift shop.

Xena, Adam, Andy outside the BRO. [RCAG]

Xena presented Christmas gifts. [RCAG]

Mike, Andy, Adam on the Shuttle to Yaki Point. [RMG]

Another benefit of Maswik is its walking-distance proximity to the Backcountry Reservations Office (BRO), where an early morning shuttle can provide

Stogie, Adam, Andy, Raudy, Xena, Mike. The shuttle dropped us off at Yaki Point, the trail head for the South Kaibab Trail. [AM]

The first steps of the hike. [RMG]

transportation to the South Kaibab trailhead at Yaki Point (from 1 hour before sunrise to 1 hour after sunset).

Raudy descends the Kaibab switchbacks. [AT]

Adam (arrow) and Mike in the upper Kaibab cliff. [RCAG]

While waiting at the BRO, Xena presented the rest of us with her backpacker-aware Christmas gifts.

It doesn't look like much snow on the ground in the Yaki Point group photo, but the upper switchbacks don't get a lot of direct sun, so the snow can be quite a bit deeper, and it can sometimes cover an ice patch on the trail. So instep crampons are always a necessity in mid-winter.

Instep crampons are quite uncomfortable when walking on pavement or on a clear, hard-packed treadway along the trail. By contrast, they fade into an afterthought when waking on crusted snow, deep snow or on ice. Good ones, with both instep and ankle straps, are stable on the boot, and resist rotating to the side of the foot, as sometimes happens with cheap "ice cleats". And they are reassuring on icy cliff trails.

We took our time in those upper switchbacks. Each of the six of us used paired trekking poles as well. In addition to the increased stability and security trekking poles offer, they are also more effective at taking stress off of the knees when stepping downward or upward. Since Grand Canyon trails are stepping up and stepping down in nearly their entirety, and having completed previous, arduous Canyon treks with only a single walking staff, I have to recommend using paired trekking poles. They allow your upper body to share

Mike, Xena, Andy, Richard, Stogie (in the lead). Hiking this was not as frightening as the photo.

[AT]

Andy.

Stogie. [AM]

South Kaibab Trail drops through Hermit shale, into the Supai. [AT]

Xena and Mike, finally out of the snow. [AM]

in the work load that would otherwise be only on your legs and knees.

As soon as the instep crampons felt unnecessary, we removed them, and tucked them away for the final climbout.

Below the icy and snowy upper trail, the hiking was the same as in summer, only colder. With exertion, our outer layers were peeled one by one. Many of the subsequent photos of our descent of the Canyon show us taking an awful lot of rest breaks, snack breaks, and breaks for any other excuse that came to mind. There was no sense in going faster than our bodies wanted us to go.

Skylight in the upper Redwall. [AT]

Views from within the Canyon are often more dramatic and more comprehensible. From the rim, the mind-numbing distances and paucity of visual references are awe inspiring. As I descend, and more rock looms above, it's easier for my mind to grasp the reality of what I'm seeing. It's similar to my intuitive grasp of the meaning of a distance to a planet, versus the distance to Flagstaff on a roadmap.

Our weather was perfect for the whole trip. But snow fell on the rims, and fog settled over side canyons. Any snow that dropped over the Canyon itself seemed to evaporate before reaching the surface. It was cold, but not too windy. So rest breaks involved doffing layers to cool down, then putting them back on again to stay warm. But I find this far preferable to hiking within the Canyon during the summer, which I have

Raudy. Note the updraft from the day's heating (white bandanna). [RCAG]

Jackets are starting to come off. [AM]

Resting at Skeleton Point hitching post. [RCAG]

Stogie. [RMG]

Xena rests. [RMG]

Raudy. [AM]

done. In summer, you can't remove enough clothing to stay cool. (On a June hike down the South Kaibab Trail in 1991, I measured 120°F a foot above the purple Hakatai shale, below the Tipoff. No lingering there.)

While backpacking in the Canyon, my body burns every single calorie it can find. I can eat healthy or eat nothing but candy bars. It doesn't seem to matter. For snacks, which restore fatigued muscles nearly instantly, I tend to carry candy bars with peanuts (and salt), beef sticks, cheese sticks (they get slimy in summer), Moose Turds, and sometimes PowerBars, though the PowerBars can be like concrete when cold, and need to be pre-warmed in a close pocket. My lunches are usually the very same stuff.

Dozing muleskinner. The mule eventually wanted to continue, so stretched its neck to pull the reins. That awakened its rider, who then resumed the climb. The mules mostly haul trash. [AM]

In addition to trash, the mule trains carry mail up from Phantom Ranch. [AM]

The mules are always interesting to observe. They seem at first to be merely passive beasts of burden. But they know their routine, and will protest when, say the lead muleskinner falls asleep, and causes the mule train to stop for too long.

A sobering thought is that, in addition to those charming, tourist mule rides, the bulk of the work that these mules carry out is to haul away the prodigious quantities of trash and garbage generated by guests and meal preparations at Phantom Ranch. There is no other way to get it out of the Canyon than by mule train. And they haul full loads of it several times every day, year round. Haul it up a mile of vertical, return down a vertical mile with groceries and supplies on the return trips. And they carry a bit of mail in both directions.

My clothing for winter Canyon treks consists of a base-layer of Thermax or polypropylene long johns and polypropylene liner socks. Although I wear Thermax briefs while hiking, because of profuse perspiration, I switch to cotton at night. My socks are thick wool (usually Smartwool "mountaineering" socks). For my upper torso, I add a fleece jacket. On top of all that, I wear a wind-proof layer of breathable nylon trousers (with removable, zip-off legs that can be partially unzipped for ventilation over my thigh muscles) and a breathable nylon jacket. I wear a ballcap for shade from sun while hiking, and always carry along a fleece or

Stogie, Adam, Andy, Xena, Mike. Every chance to rest. [RMG]

Stogie inspects a cigar (for smoking later). [AM]

Xena savors a trail snack. [AM]

Adam. [RMG]

knit sock hat, for cold hiking conditions and for a nightcap while sleeping. I carry thin, Thermax gloves, as well as windproof fleece glove that will fit over them. With all this clothing, easily removable layers is the key.

Just when the river seems really close, another switchback reveals more trail to reach it. A lot more trail.

In the photo below, we are still many hundreds of feet above the river. But with the "end" in sight for the day's hike, spirits rise.

Silver Bridge, helipad and mule corral just downriver of the mouth of Bright Angel Creek. [AT]

Andy on the South Kaibab Trail below the Tipoff. [RMG]

I believe it is important for each hiker to hike at his or her own pace. There is often a temptation to walk alongside a companion. It encourages conversation for which there is not enough surplus breath. But one of you is likely hiking too slowly to be comfortable or too rapidly to endure the pace for long. At a natural pace, a group will spread out farther along the trail, the longer the day's hike. Even when just my son and I were hiking in the Canyon for eight days (South Bass to Hermit), we would often be miles apart between rest stops, and that distance would increase as the day passed. We would, of course, rest together and camp together.

At last, we enter the short tunnel that serves as the south entrance to the Black Bridge. Even then, the bridge itself is longer than a football field.

The south end of the Black Bridge is accessed through a short tunnel in the stone. [AT]

Raudy, Xena and Mike cross the Black Bridge. The center planking is to accommodate mules. [AT]

Foundation ruins of an Anasazi pueblo near the river, between the Black Bridge and Bright Angel Creek. [RMG]

Though it boggles the mind, the Anasazi lived at the bottom of the Canyon, and apparently thrived there for nearly 3000 years, though they vanished around 1300 A.D., long before the arrival of the first Spanish explorers. We don't see any of their famous cliff dwellings in the area of the Canyon's "corridor" trails, but there are quite a few locations with ruins of their pueblo foundations and their fire pits.

There is conjecture that the climate of the inner canyon was more hospitable during their heyday, and that with long-term climate changes, they were eventually unable to maintain their communities there. Their descendants today are likely members of the Pueblo and Hopi tribes.

After snowy, icy winter on the rim, and desert most of the way down, it is always stunning to arrive at Phantom Ranch. The trees and shrubs are still green or just yellowing. It feels cozy, within the relatively close walls of Bright Angel Canyon. Bright Angel Campground is on the west side of Bright Angel Creek, and is about ¼ mile closer than the buildings of Phantom Ranch itself. There are two bridges in the area that cross the creek. One is below the campground, and the other is between the campground and Phantom Ranch proper.

Small-party campsites (by advance permit from the BRO) are first come, first served. We selected an available site, and set up camp. As the nominal trip leader, my BRO permit tag must be attached to the exterior of my backpack, and easily visible to the rangers.

I find it always a good idea to pitch my tent, and spread out my sleeping bag well ahead of turning in for the night. This allows the fill of the bag to fluff itself. All food goes into the metal ammo can provided, and packs are hung on the supporting posts.

Our tent sites in Bright Angel campground, just west of Bright Angel Creek, and south of Phantom Ranch. The cottonwood trees are still yellow in December. [RMG]

The joy of having completed the first (and most difficult for me) day of the trek was enhanced by my anticipation of a reserved steak dinner at Phantom Ranch canteen. They serve two seatings of diners each evening, an earlier steak dinner and a later stew dinner. Either one would have been ambrosia at this point. But since I knew we would be there early enough for the steak, I chose that for the first evening, and the stew for our second night there.

By the end of my first day of Canyon hiking, my legs are always rubber. They don't ache that evening. The muscles are just exhausted. I sleep like a stone, tucked into a sleeping bag, with my nightcap on my head.

It's not until the following morning that every muscle, every joint protests. Tylenol or naproxen help some.

Walking to Phantom Ranch for dinner. [RMG]

Steak dinner at Phantom Ranch. It must be ordered in advance (prior to the trip, or at Bright Angel Lodge the night before starting the hike). [RMG]

Raudy, after hiking all day downhill. Note the effort required to raise his eyebrows. [RMG]

Day 2: Layover Day at Phantom Ranch [visit Phantom Creek]

The psychological boon of a layover day is the assurance that no hiking is mandatory. I can mozy along on a "walk" of curiosity, but only if I feel like it. Morning duties are joyous, like dressing, brushing my teeth, chatting with equally content, fellow hikers. All this helps overcome the aches and pains of the morning after.

This morning was crisp and sunny. Bright Angel Creek gurgled just beyond the tents. The only pressing issue was to collect myself, so that I can head up to the canteen for breakfast—prepared by someone other than myself, and requiring no other effort than walking there and lifting a fork.

Of course, in the light of day, I had to bother with walking down to the campground's bathroom.

Stogie and Xena. Morning at the tent site. [AM]

Andy. [RMG]

Raudy walks toward the bathrooms (toilets, sinks, water) at the south end of Bright Angel Campground.   [RCAG]

I love this shot (above) of my brother walking beneath the winter canopy of Bright Angel Campground. It captures the utter loveliness of the place. To add to the charm during this particular stay there, a pair of wild turkeys had staked out their territory at the upper creek bridge, and the roofs of some of the smaller

Mike. [RMG]

Wild turkeys guard the bridge to Phantom Ranch. [AT]

Phantom buildings. They picked their fights, chasing after a timid teenager who dared to cross the bridge during their watch, but deferring to adults.

Bright Angel Creek sweeps past the campground, and separates it from Phantom Ranch. [AM]

Water in Bright Angel Creek is always cold. Even in late June, it is frigid, though welcome for a soak on a scorching day. In summer, at least, that refreshing flow comes with tiny leeches. Given the human concentration that perennially slogs about Phantom Ranch and the campground, the water is best not used —even filtered and treated—for drinking.

But the creek is gorgeous in both summer and winter, and serves to moderate both the summer heat and winter cold within the "box" of that canyon valley.

For this trek, full-fledged digital cameras were ubiquitous. Unlike previous film-camera treks, this mere four-day outing yielded over 1200 mostly stunning images from four photographers. I show only a few here.

And there were over a half-dozen short videos to boot. For previous treks, I was able to include nearly every photo. For this one, the culled photos alone could easily fill an art gallery exhibit.

Rather than the composting latrines found along some of the more popular hiking trails within the Canyon, Bright Angel Campground has actual flushing toilets in separate men's and women's bathrooms. I can only guess how their effluent is handled.

Stogie and Raudy at Bright Angel Campground. [AM]

There is one additional feature of Bright Angel Campground that may be of interest to younger, dedicated canyoneers. At the upper tent site, there is the start of a "trail" known as the Utah Flats Route. Although it is

Our tents. My tan tent was 17 years old then. [AM]

Time Warp: My same tent, finally broken, 13 years later. [RCAG]

Bathrooms at Bright Angel Campground. [AM]

not cairned, the path is visible from moderate use. It launches directly up the cliff that serves as the western boundary of the campground. It involves some difficult and scary stretches, with some exposure. Climbing that route requires roping your backpack up from the bottom. The route eventually winds its way to upper Phantom Canyon, from which it can be descended to reach Phantom Creek above a waterfall. The route must be retraced to return to Bright Angel Campground, the final descent of which is known as the Banzai Route. [Yikes!] Although I have located the start, I have never had the courage to give it a try.

After breakfast, on this layover day, we hiked up to Phantom Canyon's mouth, along the North Kaibab Trail, which involved no roping or climbing.

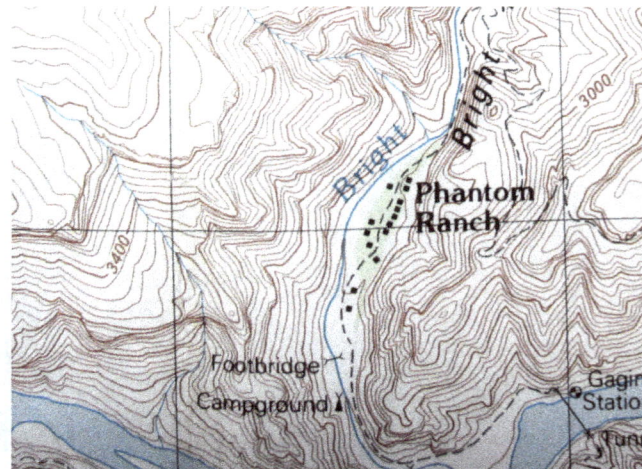
Part of the USGS 7.5 Phantom Ranch quad.

While there is a temptation to just sit and enjoy the lovely environs of Phantom Ranch, the canyon calls.

Raudy at Bright Angel campsite. [RCAG]

Phantom Ranch canteen. [AM]

Phantom Ranch

Now known as Phantom Ranch, this area along the Bright Angel delta first gained attention as a tourist camp under the name Rust's Camp. In 1902, David Rust began the planting of fruit trees and cottonwoods and the building of a camp for visitors. After Theodore Roosevelt stayed at the camp in 1913 during a hunting trip to the North Rim, the name was changed to Roosevelt's Camp. In 1922, the Fred Harvey Company commissioned Mary Jane Colter to redesign the area. She used native materials in construction and many of her buildings are in use today. At that time, Phantom Creek, a tributary of Bright Angel Creek, lent its name to the new tourist accommodations.

[AM]

Strolling to breakfast at Phantom Ranch. [AM]

Breakfast at the canteen was a peaceful, chilly, short walk from the Campground. Arriving early means standing in a queue outside the door. Since the meals are reserved in advance, the only advantage to getting there early is if a party wishes to be seated together. We waited outside for only a few minutes.

The food is generous, hearty and delicious—typical big breakfast kind of food. If you hiked down, rather than sat on a mule to get there, then the serving plates at your table will be emptied when you're done.

After breakfast, we returned to the campsite to tidy up, then hiked, pack-free, up the North Kaibab Trail, just to see the sights. The trail switches from one bank of Bright Angel Creek to the other several times along the way, traversing bridges.

What makes this additional hiking more enjoyable, other than not lugging a backpack, is that we could turn around at any point along the way. Views and perspectives are ever-changing, as the canyon narrows and widens.

We passed the intersection with the Clear Creek Trail, which I had followed solo on a previous hike. Seeing it again triggered less than happy memories of the experience.

After breakfast, hiking north on the North Kaibab Trail to Phantom Creek. [AM]

Even for a short, morning hike, we each carried water as well as a few snacks. Some brought their dual trekking poles as well. The generally northward course of the North Kaibab Trail increases in elevation as you move beyond Phantom Ranch, but the gain in this portion of the trail is not particularly tiring. And it adds to the relaxation of the return walk to Phantom Ranch. Ups and downs seldom require actually flexing one's knees, so a comfortable, level walking gait is actually a change of pace from most Canyon excursions.

Crossing one of several bridges over Bright Angel creek. [RMG]

When Adam, our one hiking companion who could lay claim to youth, caught view of the entrance to Phantom Canyon, branching off west from Bright Angel Canyon, and across the creek from the trail, he was immediately seduced. After evaluating the flow and depth of the creek at this point, he wisely chose to remove his boots, and carry them across the creek to the western bank. There, he put them back on. During his through-hike of the Appalachian Trail, he had learned the advantage of keeping one's boots dry,

Climbing Out: Grand Canyon Hikes 1997-2006

As an Appalachian Trail thru-hiker, Adam knew to remove his boots, in order to cross Bright Angel Creek, on his way to Phantom Canyon. [AM]

when needing to cross a creek or river. He wandered up Phantom Creek, beyond our line of sight.

I worry about Phantom Canyon, since it is notorious for flash floods and fatalities, even during apparently clear weather. Its hazard for surprise flooding is due to the very top of its drainage basin being quite a way up into the North Rim. A sudden downpour miles away and out of sight on the North Rim can result, soon afterwards, in a towering wall of water sweeping through Phantom Canyon. Although snow on the North Rim is far more likely in December than rain, I still worried, until Adam came back into view.

While we watched and worried, we ate our various snacks, and sipped our cold water. (Worrying is hard work.) It was a delightful morning to be casually wandering about in the inner canyon.

A curious sight along the North Kaibab Trail is the water pipeline, which carries water from Roaring Springs (way up, below the North Rim), and pipes it not only to Phantom Ranch, but also crosses the Colorado (just under the treadway of the Silver Bridge) and runs through Indian Garden and up to the South Rim. It has to suffice for hikers and millions of Park visitors every year, on both rims. But the pipeline leaks a lot, from corrosion, freezing and rockfalls. We saw several pipe joins spewing out water, just in our short walk. [Only in 2019 did the Park Service decide on an infrastructure plan to

Adam crosses Bright Angel Creek. [AM]

Adam, heading up Phantom Creek. We waited for him, until his return. [RMG]

View of the cottonwoods of Phantom Ranch, as we return south on the North Kaibab Trail. [RCAG]

Rental cabins at Phantom Ranch. [RMG]

replace the ailing water pumping station and pipelines.]

The return walk provides stunning glimpses of the precipitous, northern face of Plateau Point (a side excursion from Indian Garden) and the hazy blue South Rim, as well as the golden cottonwoods at Phantom Ranch.

We passed some of the rental cabins at Phantom Ranch, designed by Mary Jane Colter, during the 1920s, and constructed of wood and local stones. She also insisted on the name, "Phantom Ranch". They are fairly reasonably priced [even in 2019], and must be reserved in advance.

[Unlike the pricing of the charming cabins, meals at Phantom Ranch are soaring into the stratosphere. Our steak dinner, a little under $30 in 2006, is approaching $50 in 2019.]

Raudy on a rare pay phone. [AM]

Xena in the Phantom Ranch canteen. [AM]

The pay phone at phantom ranch accepts only a credit card or phone card. [My guess, and it's only a guess, is that in 2019, cell service is available in Phantom Ranch, though that may depend on the carrier.]

Mail drop box in the canteen. Mail posted here will receive a special postmark (shown red). [AM]

Although there is not a post office at Phantom Ranch, there is a tooled leather drop box for letters and postcards. These are specially marked, then transported to the South Rim by mule train daily.

Another worthwhile excursion during a layover day at Phantom is a loop hike of the dramatic River Trail, which runs along the nearly vertical cliff on the south side of the Colorado, between the Silver Bridge and the Black Bridge. Raudy and I decided to explore this trail (blasted out of the rock face in the 1930s) after lunch.

We chose to begin by crossing the Silver Bridge, hiking upriver on the trail to the tunnel entrance into the Black Bridge. Returning by then crossing the

Raudy refills drinking water outside the bathrooms at Bright Angel Campground. [RCAG]

The River Trail between the bridges. [RMG]

Black Bridge is the shortest route from there back to the campground.

Although I had crossed both the Black Bridge and the Silver Bridge on several other treks over the years, I had never ventured onto this segment of the River Tail between the Bridges. After completing the loop with a tired body, I'm happy to have decided to do it.

At several points along the cliff route, I stood and waited while Raudy hiked on, in order to snap some photos of him dwarfed by the rock face. We, naturally, carried water along.

Stogie on the River Trail. [RMG]

Raudy on the River Trail between the Silver Bridge and Black Bridge. [RCAG]

Toward the end of our loop hike, we encountered a park ranger tending to a fish weir that spanned Bright Angel Creek. Year round, they gather data on the living things within the creek.

A ranger maintains a weir in Bright Angel Creek.
[RMG]

Anti-critter gadgets at Bright Angel Campground.
[RMG]

As with every heavily used campsite within the Canyon, the Park Service provides hanging poles for suspending backpacks, as well a critter-proof ammo cans for storing all food items while using Bright Angel Campground.

Mike at the campsite. [AM]

Raudy serves up stew at the Phantom Ranch canteen. [RCAG]

The beef stew dinner at the canteen (reserved in advance) was every bit as enjoyable as the steak of the previous night. Quick-cook, dehydrated backpacking meals just can't measure up to the real deal.

We had our fill, snapped a few photos of the token Christmas decorations and lighting, then meandered back to the tent site for another night of rest. I carried a small flashlight, as well as a UCO candle lantern for use in camp at night. Raudy preferred a strap-on headlamp.

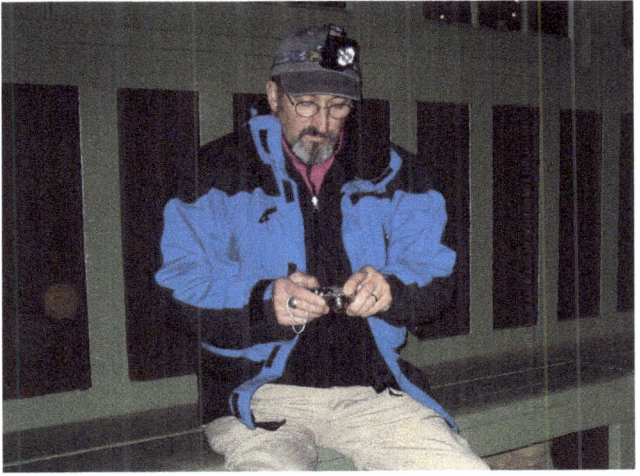

Raudy wears a headlamp, outside the canteen. [AM]

Day 3: Climbout from Phantom to Indian Garden [Bright Angel Trail]

Xena crosses the Silver Bridge to begin the climb to Indian Garden. [AT]

Two days left of this "codger hike". Today, we hiked from Bright Angel Campground up to Indian Garden. In my mind, I always consider this a short leg of the total climbout. In actuality, it is only a tenth of a mile shorter (4.7 vs. 4.8 miles) than the stretch from Indian Garden to the South Rim (9.5 mile total from the BA Campground). The entire climbout is an elevation gain of 4380 feet, of which the lower half is a mere 1320 feet, while that final day's climb is 3060 feet. So, the bottom half is nearly the same distance, but is less that a third of the elevation gain of the entire climbout.

But 1320 feet make a tiring climb up to Indian Garden nonetheless. We cross the Silver Bridge, without thinking about the arithmetic. Today will be an easier day than tomorrow.

From the photos, you can see that there was a lot of smiling happening as the day began—our easiest backpacking day of the trek. The smiles persisted to about the base of the Devil's Corkscrew.

There is no minimizing of this particular section of the climb. It was our first actual climbing of the trip. And the Devil's Corkscrew represents nearly all of the vertical gain of the entire distance between the river and Indian Garden. We huffed and puffed, spreading way apart from one another, as our differing hiking capacities came into play.

With essentially a half-day hike to Indian Garden, even the exertion of the climb didn't weigh too heavily on my mood. But I climbed slowly.

During the downhill of the first day, my overweight body took it out on my legs and knees. Now, with gravity working against me, my aerobic endurance was put to the challenge. It passed with a C-. Being, at the time of this trek, the most conspicuously overweight member of our group, I noticed my extra weight with every step.

Mike and Xena at the base of the Bright Angel Trail. [AM]

The "other" portion of the River Trail runs from the Silver Bridge, along the river, and to the base of the Bright Angel Trail. These two photos are taken at the bottom of the BA Trail, with the Silver Bridge in the distance. I believe Adam took this shot of Andy at the river, using Andy's camera, though I'm only certain that the image came from Andy's camera.

Logically, the next photo, of a smiling Adam, was simply shot by Andy from the same place, but facing away from the river, into the mouth of Garden Canyon.

Andy at the river.

Adam on the Bright Angel Trail. [AM]

The trail creeps along the sandy bed of Garden Creek for a bit, then begins its aggressive climb up through the convoluted rock of the pink and black Vishnu schist. From what I understand, the Devil's Corkscrew switchbacks its way up a steep slope of Vishnu schist rubble mixed with debris from sedimentary erosion coming from above—most likely crumbled Tapeats. The trail there is steep and serpentine. There are no exposures, as we see with cliff trails, but still with excellent vistas to reward any rest break along its tiring course.

Mike and Xena on the Bright Angel Trail. [AM]

Some of the finest views in the Canyon are from the lower Bright Angel Trail, looking toward the river while a morning haze still lingers in the Inner Gorge.

Mike and Xena on the Devil's Corkscrew. [AM]

View of the Inner Gorge, partway up the Bright Angel Trail. [AT]

Stogie rests below the Tapeats. [AT]

Some of the loveliest resting areas are to be found just

A shadow on the Bright Angel Trail. [RCAG]

Andy. [AM]

below the pie crust of the Tapeats. Truly comfy spots provide a place to stand up the backpack, and lean against it.

Regardless of the rest breaks, fatigue begins to show in everyone's face. Rather than a selfie of my tiring facial expression, I instead captured a better image of how my body was feeling—losing substance, appearing more as a shadow of the hiker I was in earlier years.

The trail continues its climb. We rest more, hike more, and move aside for descending mule trains.

I once asked a muleskinner why they preferred to use mules in the Canyon instead of horses (which are occasionally seen, mounted by their visitor-owners). "They're safer in the Canyon."

The value of high-sugar snacks is most felt during uphill climbs. Their surge of energy wakes up both the fatigued mind and fatigued muscles. And lots of water.

Raudy rests on the Bright Angel Trail. [AM]

Nothing will convince a mule to go over the cliff. Horses are not as stubborn. [AM]

Expansive prickly pear garden on the trail to Plateau Point. [AM]

Adam at Plateau Point. [AT]

I was the last member of our party to complete the day's climb. But it was still just early afternoon. After setting up camp at Indian Garden, four of us decided to hike (pack-free) out to Plateau Point, north of the Campground.

As is usual with hiking on the Tonto, it appears relatively easy and flat (by Canyon standards) from a distance. In reality it consists of a lot of short climbs and descents to cross erosion valleys and ridges. But the views from Plateau Point, even for this jaded Canyon hiker, were worth every step to get out there.

The trail to Plateau Point starts off following the Tonto Trail west for about ¾ mile, then branches northward, ending abruptly at Plateau Point after another ¾ mile. So the round trip from Indian Garden is about 3 miles. Even though it is part of the tourist corridor, it offers some of the finest views of the Inner Gorge to be found without hiking the western Tonto.

Stogie at Plateau Point. [AM]

Raudy at Plateau Point. [AM]

With many of the Canyon's spectacular viewpoints, it's tempting to be stupid, and stand in dangerous spots for a great photo. Raudy stands with no railing, but with a nearby, broader ledge behind him, and out of the camera's view. (I can't account for Adam's photo here.)

Andy at Plateau Point. [RCA]

View of the Inner Gorge and Colorado River, from Plateau Point, looking downriver.

[RCAG]

Raudy, Andy, Adam and Stogie at Plateau Point. [AM]

A photo of a group of companions together at a notable, recognizable location is what I consider a "money shot". It's the kind of photo that ends up on the wall. I really like this one. But the earlier photo taken at Yaki Point, just before we began hiking on day one shows all six of us together, and is now the framed one that I see every day.

Day 4: Climbout from Indian Garden [Bright Angel Trail]

Climbing out from Indian Garden is a generous half-day hike. It's "only" 4.5 miles to the trail head, but after the initial, gentle slope of the southern edge of the Tonto platform, the climb is nearly relentless, on switchbacks and traverses. This was my most difficult climbout ever.

But apparently I looked worse than I felt. At each rest (at least every other switchback) I would sit with my jacket off, my face red from exertion, and my cap off my head—just cooling off. Everyone passed me. And from the Redwall upward, nearly every passing hiker or small group would pause to ask if I was okay. I was

Three-Mile Rest House on Bright Angel Trail. [RCAG]

58 years old (third oldest in our group of six), was bald, with a giant, white beard, and a sweating, red face. But I really did feel okay. I just had to take it slowly.

Andy, near the top of the Bright Angel Trail.

Xena and Mike at the Bright Angel tunnel. [AM]

Climbing Out: Grand Canyon Hikes 1997-2006

Stogie was the slowest climbing out, and the last to reach the rim. Everyone else has already eaten their dinner at Bright Angel Lodge, and are now patiently waiting for him to clean his plate—which he did.

Xena at the Christmas tree in the lobby of Bright Angel Lodge. [AM]

Looking back now, at the age of 71, I see this "codger hike" as a wonderful, though modest trek with friends. My present, slimmer and more physically fit self is no longer able to backpack.

This summer (2019), my brother—Raudy, by trail name—and I drove out to the North Rim with my 12 year old grandson. We walked some of the rim trails there, and slept in tents. It was a lovely experience. But I truly miss backpacking into the Canyon.